The Centuries of Revolution

Democracy—Communism—Zionism

BY WILLIAM WHITE

PUBLISHED BY THE BARNES REVIEW 2012

The Centuries of Revolution:
Democracy–Communism–Zionism

By WILLIAM WHITE

Published by:

THE BARNES REVIEW
P.O. Box 15877
Washington, D.C. 20003

ISBN #978-1-937787-05-9

Ordering more copies:

Order more copies of *THE CENTURIES OF REVOLUTION* (softcover, 200 pages, $25 plus $5 S&H) from THE BARNES REVIEW, P.O. Box 15877, Washington, D.C. 20003. TBR subscribers may take 10% off the list price. Call TBR toll free at 1-877-773-9077 to charge copies to Visa, MasterCard, AmEx or Discover. See more products online at www.barnesreview.com.

Subscriptions:

A subscription to THE BARNES REVIEW historical magazine is $46 for one year (six issues) and $78 for two years (12 issues) inside the U.S. Outside the U.S: Canada/Mexico: $65 per year. All other nations: $80 per year sent via air mail. Send payment with request to TBR, P.O. Box 15877, Washington, D.C. 20003. Call 1-877-773-9077 toll free to charge to major credit cards. Order online at www.barnesreview.com. See a special subscription offer at the back of this volume or call toll free number above and ask for best current subscription offer.

Reproduction Policy:

Portions of this publication may be reproduced without prior permission in critical reviews and other papers if credit is given to author, full book title is listed and full contact information and subscription information are given for publisher as shown above.

Table of Contents

List of Illustrations

DEDICATION

This book is dedicated to the hundreds
of millions murdered, tortured and raped
by the advocates of Democracy,
Communism and Zionism.

—WILLIAM WHITE

THE WORLD TURNED UPSIDE DOWN

B ill White likes nothing more than to challenge authority. Often to his sorrow. In this book Bill challenges authority, all right. And he does so to his complete satisfaction, if not mine.

Here, Bill turns the world upside down. For haven't we all been taught from infancy that we live in a world of escalating progress? A world of constant improvement, demonstrated by automobiles, the availability of electricity, washing machines, television, porn-on-demand, bigger bombs to kill more people, larger warships, faster airplanes—unmanned drones to kill enemies more efficiently—even space ships to bring our "civilization" to aliens. Our masterminds can even out-guess God and change the weather. Wow!

But Bill is skeptical. This isn't progress at all, he says. No, we are not evolving to sainthood, we're devolving. We're going down, not up. We're knocking on Satan's door.

What! That's heresy. That's contrary to everything we have been taught, everything we've observed, our own experience.

But we're wrong. I've read this book and Bill is right. In a word, the human race is going to Hell.

Of course, Bill may be crazy and so may I. You are going to have to read this book before judging who is nuts—the world, you and me—or Bill White.

—WILLIS A. CARTO
February 2012

The Bolsheviks attacked Christian churches because Bolshevism was an essentially Jewish movement, and the Orthodox Church in Russia represented a bulwark against their revolutionary goals. However, Christianity, too, had once been a movement pushing the world forward into decay, breaking down the traditional polytheistic religion of the Indo-European peoples.

THE QUESTION OF REVOLUTION

Since the 17th century, the world has undergone a massive upheaval, and while the origins of the Golden Revolution that changed the system of Britain's government from a "pure" monarchy and aristocracy to include a democratic Parliament arise in the chaos that has been slowly embracing the world since the dawn of time, it is here that our story really begins, since it is here that the seeds of the modern movements of democracy and communism first took root. From the Golden Revolution the American Revolution took its inspiration, and from the American Revolution, the French Revolution, and from the French Revolution, the uprisings of 1848, the First World War, the Bolshevik Revolution, the Second World War, the war against so-called "white supremacism," particularly in the United States during the "Civil Rights Error," and the current war to transform and destroy the religion of Islam.

These revolutions are often seen as isolated events, and when they are not, they are seen as steps taken in the progress of man toward a definite, historically defined and history-ending conclusion. The idea of progress in time is not normal— the normal view of time is that it is a great destroyer, and that movement forward in time is a movement toward the destruction, not the improvement, of the beings that exist within it. The idea of revolution itself refers to the turning of a wheel, and toward a view of time that is cyclic—that the way of life of the past is simply changing to another way of life that will eventually change back into the way of life that preceded it.

What one finds when one investigates the question of the modern revolutions is that these events that have pushed both white society and the world into increasingly undifferentiated, egalitarian, anti-hierarchical and, ultimately, failed forms of social organization are not isolated, nor are they the result of an inevitable historical progress of mankind from a lower state to a higher. Instead, the revolutions that have defined human history and undermined white society are simply stages of decay on the corpse of what was once Traditional man.

Tradition is a term that is used too loosely in modern society, and is often applied to the practices of primitive remnants of humanity living in isolation from the modern world. Here, in this work, Tradition is something more—it is the way of life handed down to the Aryan people upon the creation of the white race in the garden of Scandinavia and northern Germany before the great winters and before the contemporaneous recordation of history—perhaps 32,000 years ago. Traditional society is thus the divine way of life that the white race received from the gods in its infancy, and which it was given as a mission to bring to the world for the benefit of all living creatures and the living system of the world itself.

What has happened over the past few centuries is the breakdown of this Traditional world in the way in which it was always known that the breakdown and death of both the Arya and of human happiness and society would occur. What the revolutions that have brought democracy and communism to the world represent is not the progress of humanity toward a bright new future, but the destruction and enslavement of a humanity absolutely divorced from the cultural organisms that give the lives of individuals meaning and sustenance. Decadence and degradation, not progress, are the hallmarks of advancing time, and the death of the world is what the democratic and communist revolutions discussed here represent.

What one finds when one investigates these revolutions is that they are not a will-less, natural process, but the end result of millennia of planning by a cultural organism that is essentially a bacterium on the corpse of the human race. Beginning in prehistory with the worship of demonic gods that possibly represent beings that inhabited the Earth before the ascension of man, these cults have expanded and grown to infest the entire face of the Earth, and the revolutions that define the modern world represent the ascension of these culturally poisonous organisms to positions of power in the nations whose social and political structures once served to protect the people against their influence. The breakdown of Traditional society represents the displacement of the gods of the Arya and the faith of love and life that they brought to man with the worship of death and the endless slaughter and sacrifice of humankind that the dark gods of these dark forces demand.

And it is in furtherance of this realization that the development of the occult movements around the demonic forces in opposition to the Arya form the focus of the early part of this book, as the growth of the cults of Judaism and Freemasonry and their expansion from their roots in ancient Egypt into a world-consuming cancer are examined in detail. From the worship of serpents and the wilderness and the forces of chaos that man always knew to threaten mankind, we see the development of world-threatening and world-consuming forces that have slowly and systematically swallowed all of human life, dominating every area of mankind's international activities, slowly infiltrating and taking over the economic and political systems of the world, to the point where any human being who opposes them is now tortured, degraded and murdered.

The goal of these world-destroying powers cannot be obscured, and those who try to speak of the Jews and gentiles who participate in these evil religions as members of the white race or potential comrades in the struggle against other imagined enemies are as much a part of their conspiracy against mankind as those who advocate openly for the world destroyers' gods and ideals. Humanity is dying, and it is very likely that the death of the world and the ultimate enslavement of mankind cannot be prevented. The world destroyers have gone too far and "progressed" too deeply into human institutions to be dislodged or destroyed, or to be prevented from achieving their goals of the enslavement and sacrifice of the human race to their demonic gods.

Yet there is hope for the individual Arya, as the divine souls that the gods have incarnated in this period have been selected to face the final and ultimate tests of their being, as they are left to struggle and sacrifice themselves in a conflict against pure evil which they know to be ultimately hopeless in this world— and whose promise lies only in the world of the divine, the ascension into which is the only ultimate goal of the Aryan people. The Lesser Holy War, known in Islam, is most intense in this period, when it imposes the greatest suffering, and thus the victory in the Greater Holy War becomes a challenge which can only be achieved by the greatest of the most noble souls that have been chosen to fight it.

In this spirit I investigate the Centuries of Revolution and the systematic degradation of mankind which has accompanied the rise of the Judaic, Masonic and man-oriented religions and philosophies.

THE WEED TAKES ROOT

I n writing a work of this nature, one is first struck by the enormity of the task one faces. When a friend first suggested to me to approach the subject of a general history of the role of the Jews in the world subverting revolutions that gave birth to decadent modernity, I was no less struck. The Jews have been working since ancient times—since before the historical period—to reshape the world in their image, and to create a society in which all are equally slaves before them—and they are equal to none. I was first asked to focus on the 20th century, that time where the prophecy of the Bhagavad-Gita had come true, and: "Out of the corruption of women proceed[ed] the confusion of races; out of the confusion of races, the loss of memory; out of the loss of memory, the loss of understanding; and out of this, all evil." (I, v. 41)

But I found it impossible to look at the revolutions of the 20th century outside of the context of the centuries and millennia which had preceded them—a process which brought me to the dark heart of the Jewish conspiracy itself—the demonic gods of the Jewish people and their ongoing worship by both Jews and corrupt gentiles in the modern world.

The profound destructive forces that achieved victory in the 20th century are not easily recognizable by those who were born during that period, because the world we have been born in to is so abnormal as to make abnormality seem normal. As Julius Evola noted, the state in which the world found itself after World War II, with "democracy" both victorious and defining itself as "normal," was itself a state of radical abnormality, compared to the millennia of Aryan history which had preceded it. The beginning of the century saw the final destruction of the old European monarchies; the middle of the century saw the dismantling of all European racial and national feeling; the closing years of the century saw Jewish power dominant— and all of human society in a period of decadence and decline. That these Jews, once marginalized in European society, could have achieved such power, is a testament to the greed of those Europeans and Westerners who cooperated with them, and the ruthlessness with which the Jewish people were willing to pursue their goal of hatred toward mankind.

That we would enter such an age has been known to any student of the Eddas since the first Nordic prophet told our people of the earliest teachings of the gods, and the Vala sang that: "Brothers will battle to bloody end, and sisters' sons their siblings betray; woe's in the world, much wantonness; axe-age, sword-age—sundered are shields—wind-age, wolf-age, ere the world crumbles; will the spear of no man spare the other."

Yet that the instrument of this destruction would be a series of revolutions sponsored by the people our ancestors once expelled from their society—the Jews—would have been unimaginable to our people even two hundred years ago, though even then the changes that defined the 20th century were already seeds starting to germinate among Western peoples. The extent of the transformation that the Jews have been able to create among Western and European societies in the past hundred

The Jews were once marginalized, living on the fringes of European society, and spurned by Europe's Aryan nobility. Through revolution and the overturning of the normative Indo-European social structure, the Jews have inverted this situation, making themselves the overlords of a global democratic-socialist empire whose goal is world Zionist dominion. Above, Jews await deportation from St. Petersburg, Russia, after an expulsion order by the czar.

years is almost unparalleled in the annals of human history.

And it should be remarked that these changes are revolutionary—hence our title, *The Centuries of Revolution*. The goal of the Jews in pushing the social movements we discuss—the movements for "democracy," for "communism," for "liberation" of various alleged minorities, and for internationalism in general—was always to displace the power structure that preceded it, and to break down the cultural and social institutions which had served white people so successfully since our people first began to record their own history. Fundamental to these revolutions has been a distortion—a re-mythologization, one might say—

of the historical record, in which the achievements of white people, and the nature of white society, even recent white society, is falsified, to give a brighter veneer to the new society with which the Jews have replaced the old. When one has forgotten that for millennia Europe was ruled by the best of the white race, often (though admittedly not always) for the benefit of the people, and the divides of class, sex and ethnicity were not always present, the current *status quo* of perennial struggle against the vague and undefined evils of the past becomes more acceptable. It is the inability to place current events in historical and social context that defines the mass ignorance that the Jews call education, and permits the endless "debate" and meaningless party struggles that the Jews have manufactured as modern politics.

But the party cannot go on forever, and as the 20th century closed, the seeds of the destruction and economic decline that have defined the world of the 21st century were apparent. Internationalism had been victorious in the struggles of the 20th century, but with internationalism had come a series of social and economic difficulties that could not be resolved within the internationalist framework. Opposition to racism sounded good in principle, as did open borders, but the real impact of mass immigration on Western society was not precisely what those who had imposed it had promised. Further, the development of a credit culture, a natural result of the imposition of international finance, and of the welfare state, which had originally been imposed to solve the problem of non-productive minorities in white nations, had combined to hollow out the productive base of the nations the Jews were feeding upon. The manufacture of a war on terror served to provide cover for the export of the "democratic" revolution to the Muslim World, but the cost of the wars that would follow would bankrupt the nations waging them—and create instability in the international system the Jews had manufactured. Lastly, the emergence of the Internet, which saved the stagnating economy of internationalized America in the end of the 20th century, is challenging the media machines that the Jews have created to maintain support for their ideology among their hosts.

The 20th century marked the triumph of democracy, communism and Zionism over the old systems of the Western World, and the culmination of 200 years of revolutionary change in Europe. However, that triumph only allowed the victors to place the bankruptcy of their system on display, and the triumph of international Judaism opened the door for a century of international economic and social decline—decline that was already robust by the end of the century of revolution. This book is intended as a history of the social decline that accompanied the rise of Judaism, and as a warning to future generations that will be faced with the parasitism of this people, a plague all peoples have had to suffer through for millennia. In a sense, this history is an inoculation against the Jewish bacillus—a vaccine for those who may pick it up someday in the future and recognize they are facing the same problems that the West faced during the Jewish ascension. The Jews are masters at denial—"The Jew cries out in pain as he slaps you," as the Polish proverb says—but with the preservation of real history comes the preservation of real awareness, and a message to the future: Do not do what we did. Do not welcome this people into your midst. Do not allow their weed to take root. Do not allow their poison to spread.

The goat-god is often associated with Satanism and the pentagram, but the goat is a symbol of the wilderness, and the true god of the wilderness is the Jewish deity Yahweh/Jehovah, in the aspect he borrowed from the Egyptian chaos-god Seth. Yahweh/Jehovah and Satan are one and the same god.

CHAPTER ONE

THE ORIGINS OF
THE JEWISH PEOPLE

The Jews are a people who like to keep their true origins cloaked in mystery. Their mythology defines themselves as an "eternal people," a "chosen people," a people created by god for a specific purpose, and thus, unlike all other peoples, a people outside of the course of history, created at the beginning, to be with the world until the end. As with all Jewish lies and myths, the truth falls somewhat short of their ideal. The Jews are a people in time—some would say the paragon of people within time—and, as such, as with all peoples, they have a beginning and, hopefully, will have an end.

A revisionist historian I know is a strong proponent of the theory that the Jews originated from the Neanderthals, and that they represent a lower stage of evolutionary development than that of Cro-Magnon man. According to this theory of development, the two major groups of the Jewish people, the Ashkenazim and the Sephardim, emerged from the Caucasus Mountains to the plains of eastern Europe and the coast of Palestine in the third millennium B.C., representing a "lost tribe," so to speak, of the Neanderthals that had preceded them.

I disagree with this thesis, and tend to adhere to the theory put forward most notably by Carleton Coon, one of the great proponents of the idea of separate development of the human races. In the modern development of Coon's theory, the white race is derived largely from the Neanderthals, whereas the Asian race is derived largely from *Homo erectus*, and the black race largely from the pre-human Australopithecus. Since I began writing of this book, the *Journal of Molecular Biology* has come forward with new evidence that tends to support this hypothesis, noting that all of the peoples of the world share the DNA of the Neanderthal except for the Negro race, which owes its depraved state and its intellectual and immunological inferiorities to the lack of Neanderthal genes. This new research confirms what was discovered 10 years ago in DNA laboratories —that the Negro race is genetically distinct from the species we call *Homo sapiens*—and expands on it to let us know of the reason for the differences. That the Neanderthal transformed himself 32,000 or so years ago into the race we know as the white race is thus no surprise—at that time the spark that lifted men from animals to humanity was passed down and taken up by the white human race.

In modern genetic terms, we call these three races the L, M and N haplogroups, corresponding to the black, yellow and white races, and recognize that, of the six L-haplogroup sub-races, L1-L6, only one, L3, the Ethiopian, has any traits in common with the M and the N. This is almost certainly the result, as we shall discuss, of settlement by whites and Asians of the African East coast. Otherwise, there are 2,200 known points of genetic difference between the white and yellow, on the one hand, and black races, just as there are 900 known points of difference between the white and the yellow races.

In a world in which history is generally presented as certainty, and in which human knowledge is presented as having mastered every nook and cranny of what is possibly known, the limits of human knowledge, not only about science and the known mysteries of the physical universe, but about mankind itself and our own history, often escape us. In opposition to the truth of the separate racial and genetic natures of the races, we are told with great certainty that "modern man" developed 200,000 years ago, or 600,000 years ago, or 2 million years ago, but we are not told about the speculative guesswork that goes into such pronouncements, or that the "modern men" which are found are certainly not white modern men—they are Negroes or proto-Negroes, most of them developed little from their admittedly not human, ape-like ancestors. In fact, the broad definition which science has recently given to the physiognomy of "modern man" is not only a direct product of the kind of revolution we shall discuss here, but is also an indicator to how primitive some specimens of the Negro race continue to be today.

To say that the white race is derived from the Neanderthal is not to deny the Jews their genetic uniqueness, or to pretend that the Jews are properly a part of the white race. The Jews, particularly the Kohanim that have ruled over them for the past three millennia, are also known to be genetically distinct—whether through inbreeding or through some separate pre-human origin—and there is no intention here of including them in the white race. Even if their physical form was not a parody of white humanity, their spiritual form is so different that no commonalty between the Aryan and the Jew can be found.

No less a person than Friedrich Nietzsche believed that the Jews are first known to history in the Vedas, the collection of Aryan works that formed the basis of what later became the Hindu and Buddhist religions, and a close relative of both the Nordo-Germanic and Iranian pagan faiths. The Chandala, in the Vedic faith, are the caste that is so low they are assigned the unclean task of disposing of corpses, and are "people of evil conduct [who have entered] a foul womb." As Nietzsche tells us, they are "the unbred man, the mishmash man . . . the *counter-movement* to any morality of breeding, of race, [or] privilege."

But the Chandala are also something more. They are a people who were known to the early Aryans, addressed in the Law of Manu, as a race that was encountered and subjugated during the great migration of the eastern Aryan peoples into Iran and the Indian subcontinent. Building on the researches of Louis Jacoillot, it is clear that this raceless Chandala underclass was the "root race" of the Hebrew people.

The Aryan peoples—those people who threw out three branches from Central Asia in the period 2200 to 1700 B.C., and who founded civilizations in Persia, India, the Near and Middle East and even Celtic and southern Europe—arrived in Central Europe, likely from Scandinavia and northern Germany, before 4500 B.C., possibly as early as 6000 B.C. Generally, they appear to have been what is called the Kurgan culture, and which is known throughout the Eurasian steppes, into the Balkans, Anatolia and the Danube. They are known from the archeological record in the foot-lands of the Himalayas by 4000 B.C., and it has long been believed that modern Tajikistan was one of the centers of Aryan civilization (the foothills of the Ural Mountains and the Oxus-Jaxartes river basins by the former Aral Sea being the others). Not surprisingly, modern Tajikistan is also believed to have been a major center, if not the center, of Neanderthal civilization, perhaps 25,000 or more years before the Aryans.

The Chandala theory further accords with what is known of the historical Jewish people. The Bible tells us that Abraham came from Ur of Chaldea (Ur Kasdim), and while the location of this Ur is debatable, many have placed it in "Shinar," and have identified Shinar as Sumeria—the southern portion of Mesopotamia, modern-day Iraq. Many believe that the Jews, like

Friedrich Nietzsche was the first to connect the Jewish people with the Chandala outcastes of Aryan India. While the Jews claim to be a timeless people with origins in Palestine and the Arabian peninsula, the truth is that they are, like all peoples, a transient grouping in mundane historical time.

the Sumerians before them, migrated to this area from the east, and the path of migration from the east into southern Mesopotamia is generally one that begins in central Asia, near Tajikistan. It should be noted that an alternative theory places Ur in northern Mesopotamia, between Assyria and Aram, suggesting an initial origin of the Jews in the deserts of Arabia.

But there is also genetic evidence to support a claim of migration. A 2005 article in the *Journal of Genetic Genealogy*, "A Mosaic of People: The Jewish Story and a Reassessment of the DNA Evidence," stated "modern Jews exhibit a diversity of genetic profiles, some reflective of their Semitic/Mediterranean ancestry, but others suggesting an origin in European and Central Asian groups." The Jews as a people are not genetically homogeneous, but certain castes within Jewry are, particularly the Kohanim—or Jews who have the last name of Cohen—and the Levites. This mixed racial composition combined with a genetically unified ruling caste conforms to what is known of the Jews as they first become known to history—as the Habiru.

The Habiru (Egyptian Apiru) are generally believed to be the Hebrew people, though there has also been a movement to resist this identification among Jewish scholars. These people first emerge in history about 1800 B.C., when a king of Yamkhad, modern Aleppo, Syria, is said to have made peace with the leaders of the Habiru. The Habiru developed trade routes between the cities of Syria and Palestine and those of the Mesopotamian river valleys and eventually became a pawn in the game of chess played between the Hittite and Egyptian empires. In this context, they are known from their invasion of southern Canaan during the reign of the Egyptian Pharaoh Akhenaton, during the 14th century B.C., an act which likely confirms to the return of Isaac into the land of Canaan, before the Exodus and the conquest of the region.

Some background to the world of the 14th century B.C. may be helpful. In the world of the 14th century, there were two major powers fighting for what is now Palestine—the Egyptian empire and the Hittites. Other powers, particularly the Semitic kingdom of Assyria and the Hurrian-speaking nation of the Mitannis, existed, but the Hurrians—and the Hittites who conquered Mitanni—acted as a buffer against Assyrian influence in Palestine. The Egyptians were composed of two peoples, the northern Semitic peoples, who inhabited the Nile Delta—the area known biblically as Goshen—and the southern peoples, likely of proto-Aryan descent. Both had inhabited that land since before 3000 B.C. The Hittites were relative newcomers to the region and had invaded Asia Minor across the Caucasus Mountains, along with the other Indo-European peoples of the Near and Middle East, before 1800 B.C., when they founded the Hittite Old Kingdom. Prior to the Old Kingdom, Anatolia had been economically dominated by Semites from Assyria—Semites whose power collapsed when the Hurrians conquered their trade routes and allowed the Hittites to declare independence.

As the world entered the 14th century B.C., the Hittites had just reunified their empire, and were waging war against the Mitannis, who were their traditional enemies in the region. In

Egypt, a social crisis was brewing as Pharaoh Akhenaton, believed to be of mostly Aryan ethnic origin, attempted to suppress the cult of Amun, which owned much of the land of Egypt and had come to dominate the Egyptian religious system. Between the two empires was the land the Egyptians called Eham, biblical Canaan, which was ruled by a smattering of small princes who dominated local city-states. Since the foundation of the 18th Dynasty, of which Akhenaton was a part, the Egyptian empire had dominated the Hamitic princes of modern Palestine, and held them in tribute. But the Hittites wanted control of the region so as to make an end-run around the fortifications the Mitannis had built along their border.

The result was a series of wars in Canaan in which a prince named Aziru consolidated the northern part of the country while the people known as the Habiru overran and butchered the inhabitants of the southern part—what would later become Judea. Busy with civil disturbances and religious reformation, Akhenaton was unable to intervene—and from the letters that were sent to him from his subject princes, we know the name and the nature of the people the Egyptians called the Apiru.

The Apiru were nomadic. *The Oxford Biblical History* tells us they were "a loosely defined, inferior social class composed of shifting and shifty population elements without secure ties to settled communities." One modern Jewish scholar, David Silverman, describes them as "a social class of mafia-like brigands." Yet their Egyptian name means "the equipped," "the knowledgeable" or "the initiated," and they seem to have formed a secret society operating within the context of the Egyptian and Semitic nations.

Whether the Apiru were Semites is an open question. Semite means "descendent of Shem," and is part of the Biblical racial schema described in Genesis 10. However, the term "Shemu" is Egyptian, like "Eham," and is used to describe the people of the Egyptian northern delta region. The Apiru, or Habiru, people seem to have had ethnic ties to the people of the northern part of the fertile crescent, and all of these people are known to have dwelt in northern Egypt, Syria and northern Mesopotamia as early as 3000 B.C. They are believed to have emerged from the Arabian desert. The Hebrews are simply not known in the region prior to 1800 B.C., when they are seen attacking the town modernly called Aleppo and are thus placed firmly in the area of the Near East inhabited by Semites. The evidence, though, is that the Hebrews are a people who came to the Semitic portion of the Near and Middle East long after the Semitic people had migrated or conquered there, and interbred with the people we now know as Arabs, rather than being genetically cognate with them.

It may have been when the Apiru entered into Egypt that they developed their Semitic identity—an event that occurred much as the Old Testament tells us. The details the Bible provides of their travails in Goshen are of interest, because we see a pattern emerge that dogs the Hebrews throughout the next three and a half millennia of their existence. In the Biblical story of Joseph, the Hebrew works his way up from prisoner to advisor to the pharaoh on the strength of his ability to interpret dreams. Joseph predicts, correctly, seven years of plenty followed by seven years of famine.

But what is done with this knowledge is interesting—Joseph spends seven years hoarding up all the grain of Egypt, appropriating the labor of the farmers and peasants over whom he rules, and, when the famine comes, he does not give the grain back to the people, but sells it to them, and sells it to them not only until he possesses all the people's money, but until he possesses their livestock, their real estate, their means of production, and, eventually, their liberty. This continues until a pharaoh emerges who does not know Joseph, and who commits the terrible crime of forcing the Jews to work for a living, against which the Jews rebel, creating the Exodus.

That the Exodus from Egypt was a historical event that oc-curred in the 12th century B.C., and which was recorded no later than the 11th century B.C., is a virtual certainty, particularly because of the evidence given us in the Bible. The racial schema we receive from Genesis 10 is that of the world of the Egyptian and Hittite empires of the 13th and 12th centuries B.C. The opening chapter of Genesis, the first creation saga, is derived from a Sumerian poem of great antiquity, and portions of the Bible are derived from Egyptian poems and literary works as late as the reign of Akhenaton in the 13th century. Further, Egyptian words occur in the names and eponyms of the rulers and ancestors of the Hebrews up until the end of the monarchy of Saul. Most of the Hebrew culture that has been passed down to the modern world through the Bible is the Egyptian culture of the late New Kingdom combined with the religious views of the Philistine Sea Peoples that attacked Canaan in the late 13th and early 12th centuries.

Of particular interest for our purposes is the adoption of the Egyptian god Seth by the Jews, as it is the worship of this deity and his associates around which the Hebrew and modern Jew-ish religion coalesced. Seth was the god of the Semites of Goshen, and, as the Jews dwelled among them, it is not sur-prising that they adopted his worship as their own. In the Bible, Seth appears as a late brother of Cain and Abel, and is the founder of the line of Hebrew patriarchs before Noah. Since the earliest times in Egypt, Seth had been seen as a chaotic deity opposed to the order represented by Re and Osiris. He was the deity of the wilderness and of the area of Isfet—lawlessness—outside of the world of Ma'at represented by the Nile Valley. He is associated with wild animals, such as the hippopotamus—later the goat in northern nations without hippopotami—and was portrayed as an enemy of Horus, the Aryan storm god of the southern Egyptian kingdom. Efforts were made to repair Seth's image over the years, but after the time of the Hyksos, a foreign people who conquered Egypt in the 18th century B.C., until the Rammesside pharaohs, Seth was considered a definite enemy of Egyptian society.

As such, it should be no surprise that, during their time in Egypt, the Jews adopted the worship of Seth as their own. Seth was identified by the Egyptians with two other deities—the Egyptian serpent demon Apep, and the Syriac god Baal. In fact, Seth and Baal are used interchangeably in Hebrew names as late as the line of Saul, perhaps in the 11th century B.C.

Apep was a serpent who lived in the underworld and struggled each day to prevent the sun from rising. Originally, Seth was allied with Re, the sun god, in the struggle against Apep. However, the Hyksos had such a hatred of Egypt that they elevated Apep to their national god, and even named their kings after him. During their reign, Apep and Seth became syncretized into one being.

As Seth was a wilderness god, and Apep a fire-breathing serpent of the underworld, Baal was the god of the destructive power of the storm. Originally, perhaps, a positive storm figure, he is first known to us among the Semitic peoples who conquered Sumeria, where, like Seth in the Old Kingdom mythos, he is the slayer of the underworld serpent Tiamat. Baal's nature changed though over the centuries, like Seth's, and as his worship spread over the world (eventually reaching both Britain and Scandinavia) he became identified with roaring beasts, whose growls reminded men of the roaring of the wind.

These symbols of these three gods were often combined by the Egyptians into a single beast—Amemet—who had the head of a lion, the body of a serpent, and the rear parts of a hippopotamus. Amemet's function was to eat the corpses of those who were found unworthy by the judgment of Osiris in the underworld after their death. Later, the hippopotamus became represented by a goat, as one encountered wildernesses in which hippopotami did not dwell, and the beast became the one known to classical myth as the chimera.

This three-headed beast—the god of the wilderness, of the fiery serpent and of the destructive storm—became adopted by the Jews as Yahweh-Jehovah, and all three aspects are found in his story. The Jews enter the wilderness because it is sacred to their god, who protects and feeds them there, while later making them prey to wild beasts when they anger him. The fiery serpent is found in the serpentine powers of Moses, and in the fiery mountains that consume the Jews' enemies. The god of the storm and wilderness is found in the lightning, brushfires and dark clouds that define Yahweh's form. The god the Jews chose to worship is a composite of the forces of chaos, death and destruction that they encountered during their time among the Egyptian peoples.

Later, this deity came to be known as Moloch or Baal Haamon, and an effort was made by a segment of Jewish society to reject it in favor of another god well known in the eastern Mediterannean—IOVE—the deity whose name the Jews transliterated as YHWH.[1] Both became identified with the possibly Egyptian god Amun, and Baal became worshipped in many Semitic nations as Baal Hammon, while the Mycenaean Greeks, in ignorance, found an aspect of their storm god Zeus in Zeus Ammon. Yet the worship of Jove, whom the Romans associated with Jupiter, did not enlighten the Jews, but rather was corrupted by syncretism with their demonic god, who retained his essential character as a hodgepodge of world-destroying Egyptian demons.

The time of the Exodus to the time of the Babylonian captivity, about 1200 B.C. to 586 B.C., is a formative period in Jewish history, best known through the Bible. The Jews, like many contemporary people, practiced human sacrifice, the "dooming to destruction" so often mentioned in Biblical texts, such as Leviticus 27 (though the specific nature of what occurred to humans "dedicated" to Yahweh is obscured in many translations), and the initial entry of the Jews into Canaan appears to have been accompanied by the ritual human sacrifice of entire cities, in a way the Semitic Assyrians would parallel in the 10th through 8th centuries B.C. But after gaining power, and dividing their land into the kingdoms of Judea and Israel, the Jews calmed down and played a much lesser role in world affairs. They adopted the relatively peaceful religions of the golden calf and Asherah—the religion of the Great Mother as Isis-Hathor— as reactions against both Yahweh-ism and the worship of Baal and Baal Haamon, the demon Moloch.

The Old Testament also undergoes several revisions during this period, the original text being altered several times to conform to the demands of the Aaronid priesthood and the adherents of Moses, which formed rival factions among the Jews. The Deuteronomist text—the lengthy compendium of laws that also includes Leviticus—was likely "discovered" in order to restore national unity to the people of Judea following the destruction of Israel/Samaria by Assyria, and while there was a definite priesthood which controlled and manipulated the Jewish kings, the people of Judea were not as plagued with the quibbling of rabbis as they (and the world) are today.

What changed this state of relative peace was the Babylonian conquest, in which a brief resurgence of Chaldeans in Mesopotamia, newly liberated from the defeated Assyrians, allowed a Babylonian empire to flash up and consume the Near East, including the weakened and impotent Jewish state. Jerusalem was destroyed, and the Jewish people were taken into Babylon as slaves, where they would remain for about 50 years.

About 536 B.C., Babylon was conquered by a resurgent Per-

sian empire, and the Persian empire was petitioned by a segment of the captive Jews, known as the Ezraites for their adherence to the priest Ezra, to allow their return to Jerusalem. Cyrus,
the Persian emperor, agreed and allowed the Jews in Babylon
the choice to either return to Palestine or to stay where they
were. Most of the Jews opted to stay, but the Yahwehites, the fa-
natical priesthood that had dominated the old monarchy of
Judea, opted to return, and did return—receiving a subsidy
from the Persians to rebuild their shattered city and temples.

This return from Babylon was the foundation of the modern
Jewish people. Ezra and his Jewish disciples authored the final
recension of the Bible upon their return, restoring some of
Moses's role in the Exodus and putting the final dots on the i's
and the crosses on the t's of what is now the modern biblical
text. They also firmly established Yahweh in the place of what
had been the popular religion, the worship of Isis, the golden
calf. They also began a process of Hellenization, in which they
syncretized their religious system with that of the increasingly re-
gionally dominant Greek peoples, most importantly identifying
their god Yahweh with the Greek god Typhon, a fire-breathing
underworld serpent demon who rebelled against the gods and
lies under the earth waiting to rebel again—the model of the
modern Christian Satan. From no later than the fourth century
B.C., depictions of Yahweh as a chicken-headed, man-bodied
demon with each leg a serpent are found on Jewish medallions.
This faction of Jewry became the biblical Sadducees.

In the late 4th century, Judea was absorbed by the Macedon-
ian empire, and the Hellenization process was completed—
though, it is interesting to note, Judea was one of the few
provinces of Alexander's Macedonia not to accept and adopt
the worship of Serapis, which Alexander had conceived of as a
religion for all the world. In reaction to the Sadducees, awaken-
ing the age-old conflicts within the Jewish people over the man-

ner in which their religion should be worshipped, and the manner in which it should be understood in relation to the outside world, arose the Pharisees. The Pharisees were a group of priests, in contrast to the Sadducees, who believed that, along with the text of the Torah, the oral teachings of Jewish rabbis, what later became the Talmud, should be considered as holy writ, and foreign elements, such as the Greek syncretisms and the Egyptian origins of their religion, should be extirpated.

Judea was located at a crossroad of several empires. It was vassalized by several of the nations which emerged from Alexander's empire, and was eventually absorbed by Rome. It was during the period when it was conquered by Rome that the Jews again became international in their outlook. There was a fierce Jewish nationalism, which saw in its struggle against Roman domination the struggle of the serpent Typhon against the god of order, Jupiter, but there was also a segment of the Jewish people that was attracted to the centers of Roman power, and which gravitated toward the Roman capital. When Rome descended into anarchy, and its republican government collapsed under the strain of foreign wars and became the empire, this faction of Jews attempted to influence the imperial line, sending its daughters as whores and its sons as advisors to seduce the emperors and influence their counsel.

During the Roman occupation, a prophet emerged in Judea that we now know as Jesus Christ, and the religion he taught provided one of the greatest challenges the Jewish people were to face. Needless to say, the Jews went all out in an offensive to suppress the growing Christian faith as heresy. Under the influence of a Jewish seductress, the Emperor Nero, for instance, ordered Christians burned as torches to light his festivities, and others ordered Christians slain by exposure to wild beasts. Some even say the New Testament was written during this period by a group of Romans opposed to Nero, including Seneca and Lucius Piso, who derived it from Aryan mythical stories.

The spread of Christianity, originally viewed as a sect of Judaism, later seen as so dangerous to the Roman form of government that it was co-opted by the Roman empire, eclipsed Judaism's activities during much of the first century of Christ's era, yet the Jews did not disappear. Under the Roman empire, they spread throughout the provinces of Rome, and retained their power in the Near East, where the constant wars between Rome and Persia provided opportunity for smuggling and trade. Jewish nationalism rose at times against the Roman empire, such as in the rebellion that Titus Flavius crushed, burning the Second Temple of Solomon in A.D. 70. But the Jews acted more as a secret force, infiltrating Roman ruling circles, as in the case of the Jew Josephus, and passing off their pseudo-learning as wise counsel, and their schemes as shrewd politics.

After the destruction of the temple, the Sadducees, who had controlled the temple offices, essentially dissolved as a Jewish power faction, and the Pharisees consolidated their hold on power, writing down the doctrines taught by their rebbes and publishing the documents that became known as the Talmud, as well as several of the major collections of Jewish folklore and mystical tales that are the foundation of modern Judaism as it is practiced today.

With the fall of the Roman empire in the west, the Jews found themselves governed by German tribes, which they despised, not least of all because the Christianized Germans had no tolerance for their Hebrew tricks. In the east, the rise of Islam provided new opportunities for the Jews, who capitalized upon Islam, after initially resisting it, by taking positions in the government of the caliphs as viziers and helping lead the Islamic conquest of the Near East, Africa and southern Europe. The two tendencies came together when the Jews opened the gates of the Gothic kingdoms in Spain, ending German rule in Hispania for several centuries.

As the great hordes of Asia invaded eastern Europe, one eastern European people, of Turkish, or central Asian, origin, converted to Judaism: the Khazars. The Khazars, trapped between the empires of the Islamic and Catholic world, chose what they thought was the "middle road" of Judaism, and were accepted by the Sephardic Jews of the Middle East as kinsmen. These Khazars formed the Ashkenazic branch of Jewry—the majority of the Jews alive today—and had no ethnic relationship to the Hebrews of the Bible, as modern genetic tests have confirmed.

The Khazar empire persisted on the plains of modern Ukraine for several centuries before it was destroyed in a holy war by Sviatoslav I of Kievan Rus.' Sviatoslav, a semi-mythical Nordic-Slavic hero, was a member of the Russian dynasty of Novgorod who, not satisfied with merely raiding the Jewish cities of the Caspian, resented Jewish control over Russian trade with Mesopotamia and the Near East, and determined to not only seize the trade routes, but smash the Jewish empire so it could never recover. In the 10th century, Sviatoslav invaded and destroyed Khazaria in a five-year war that burned and razed most of the major Khazar cities, their population put to the sword. However, after smashing the empire and gaining his objectives, he failed to destroy several Khazar successor states that emerged in the Caucasus Mountains —and thus the Ashkenazic Jews were able to regroup and re-enter Europe in the second millennium after Christ.

This Jewish migration into eastern and northern Europe, and from there into France and Britain, prompted the various medieval laws against Judaism and Jewish trading. The primary role the Ashkenazim took upon themselves was that of middleman between goods manufactured in the nations of Poland, eastern Europe and Germany, and all of the nations where they settled. They would convince the Germans the Polish version of the goods the Germans produced domestically was superior, and the Poles that the German versions of the same goods were superior, and would trade goods between the nations, taking a percentage for their "middleman" role, and producing or contributing nothing of value.

The Jews also used their profits to become great usurers in Europe, lending money at interest, much in the way Isaac had among the Hittites during their ancestors' time in Palestine. The Torah says that Isaac "sowed his fields," and they returned to him a hundred fold, and the fields he sowed were the gullible goyim, who took his seed—his money—at high interest rates, and ended up in such deep debt that the interest he collected was more than a hundred times the capital he had lent.

This behavior led to the anti-Jewish movements and occasional purges of the late first and early second millennia A.D. Another factor was the continued involvement of some Jews in ritual human sacrifice, a practice well documented across Europe, though the degree to which its practitioners were in a minority among the Jewish people is open to debate. Being bound under the Noahide laws to dedicate to destruction any people who did not follow the Jewish religion, and to sacrifice their victims to Yahweh by draining them of blood, and then consuming the tenth portion of the flesh, many Jews kidnapped children and murdered them during this period. In part, occult movements that developed among Jewish rabbis played a role, including movements centered around documents like the Zohar, which alleged to contain magic formula for amulets and medallions, many created out of the blood of innocents.

Simultaneous with these Jewish occult movements developed a gentile occult movement built out of opposition to Christianity and an embrace of Catholic notions of demon worship, loosely based in pagan tradition. The most significant of these occult movements was that of the "master masons of

Baal," which developed from the association of the Biblical demon Baal with "sorcery" that incorporated memories of the worship of Egyptian Seth, as well as the nation of Persia and Hebraic tales of the Tower of Babel. What learned Catholic scholars had come to believe during the dark ages, in part based upon a misreading of Pliny and of the Trojan epilogues, was that a sorcerer named Zoroaster, who was also Baal, had contracted 72 master masons to build the Tower of Babel, and that this Zoroaster and his masons had been the masters of sorcery.

From this doctrine emerged the sect of Freemasons, who would work with the Jews throughout the second millennium after Christ to dismantle the traditional institutions of Europe and replace them with the chaos of democracy. Baal, known in Nordic countries under names like Bel, Beli and Billing, was a storm god, the god of the howling wind, who was associated with chaos, wild beasts, intoxication, sex, cannibalism and murder, and his adherents believed in creating a new world order, with themselves at the top, based upon the liberation of the masses. Because healthy society depended upon hierarchy and order, the destruction of class and caste differentiations through the leveling and equalization of man created unhealthy and chaotic societies, where individuals were rootless and blown about like the storm represented by their god.

In the 11th and 12th century, the Freemasonic movement infiltrated the Catholic knightly orders that were attacking Islamic rule in the Holy Land, gaining control of the Knights Templar, and eventually other groups. Like the Jews, the Masons, through these initiatic orders, set up international banking and trading empires, as well as funding heretical movements in Europe designed to draw people into their form of demon worship. Though the Knights Templar were crushed by the Catholic Church, their base of La Rochelle in France remained a center of their occult movement, and their organization retained bridgeheads in Scotland and elsewhere.

Of all the expulsions of the Jews which occurred during this period, the most important occurred in Spain, where Ferdinand and Isabella, having seen the cooperation of the Jews with Spanish Christendom's Islamic enemies, ordered all Jews to abandon their property and the country. Many Jews did, fleeing primarily to Amsterdam and to Venice, though many remained as "conversos," continuing to subvert the crown, and leading to the inquisition. Ironically, the inquisition was led by a converted Jew, Tomas de Torquemada, as was much of the "Catholic" persecution of the Jewish people. As they would into modern times, the Jews took extreme positions on both sides of an issue—even when the issue was opposition to Judaism—in order to ensure the survival of their people.

The actions of the inquisition turned the Jewish people against Catholicism permanently, and Freemasonry and Judaism came together in the mid-second millennium in the form of the Reformation and Renaissance, in which the by then traditional institution of the Catholic Church was dismantled for the primary purpose of establishing occult "democratic" rule in its place. The appeal of what became known as Protestantism was in the national desire of the northern and German peoples. The Holy Roman Empire, which had been a Germanic empire since its founding by Charlemagne, represented the ideal of the Germanic people united against the southern, Near-Eastern-izing force of Catholic Christianity. This conflict reached its head in the Guelph-Ghibelline crisis, where the church forced the emperor into submission. But the national desires of the northern European peoples was corrupted during the Reformation as occultists, both Masonic and rabbinical, infiltrated the Protestant movement, bringing with them their own anti-Catholic and anti-Christian goals, and turned the revolt against the church into an anti-European force.

Protestant movements became viciously anti-aristocratic, attacking not only the church hierarchy, but also the European nobility, particularly in Scotland and parts of Germany, as well as France. The role of Freemasonry in Scotland, Germany, and, eventually, England, is well documented. The Whig Party in Britain was essentially a Freemasonic party, as was much of the movement against the church in southern Germany and in France. In France in particular, the effort against the crown was led by Masonic lodges, and, to combat these anti-Catholic secret societies, the church instituted the Society of Jesus (Jesuits), an anti-Masonic secret society. As with the inquisition, the founder of the Jesuits, Ignatius of Loyola, was a converted Jew.

Thus the Jews sat on both sides of an occult war which they waged successfully against the church, and which they just as successfully turned into a war against the European aristocracy who, to protect their people from the practice of usury and from cultural subversion, had restricted the anti-social activities of the Jewish people. A series of revolutions, beginning in the mid-17th century, were begun—and these revolutions formed the foundation of the Century of Revolution which the Jews would unleash upon the world in the 20th century.

First was the overthrow of King Charles I of Britain during the civil wars of 1642-1649, which has been interpreted several ways, but appears to have been a reaction against Charles's efforts to eliminate Freemasonic influence over the House of Stuart. James I, a Scotsman and Freemason, had gained control of the British crown in 1603. He was a bisexual who practiced demonic rites, and the sexual patterns of his children indicate he likely molested them. There was a struggle among his children and relatives after his death that focused on the issue of whether to continue Masonic rule or to return rule to the church, and Charles I was seen as pro-Catholic, particularly after marrying a Catholic princess. The pro-Masonic and pro-Jewish forces thus determined to overthrow Charles, and did so by propagandizing against him as a "tyrant" and demanding "freedom of religion," primarily for Masonic-controlled Protestant sects that originated in Scotland. Charles's enemies also received financial support from the Jews. Thus, when Charles was eventually overthrown, his successor, Cromwell, rescinded the edict of Edward I expelling the Jews and invited the rabbis from Amsterdam who had financed him to set up shop in England. From there, the British ruling class then helped the Jews break the Netherlands away from Catholic Spain, again in the name of Protestant Revolution. Not surprisingly, the Netherlands soon became a major exporter of dirty books and anti-Catholic religious tracts.

The second major revolution achieved by the Jews and Freemasons was the American Revolution, where the British colonies were persuaded to revolt against the crown, and the "parliamentary" reforms of the Glorious Revolution were turned into the "democratic" forms of the American republic. Rome was still a cornerstone of European thinking, but a very different kind of Roman-ism from that of the Holy Roman Empire influenced American thought. Instead of the Rome of Caesar, an idealization of the Rome of Brutus's ancestors, and the revolutionary act of Brutus in slaying Caesar, became popular. America was designed as an imitation of the Roman republic, and it was the first white nation of any significance to be ruled without a nobility—or with a nobility comprised almost entirely of Freemasons.

The third revolution was that of France, which occurred from 1789 to 1792, when Masonic cultists, working with proto-communist factions of the "Paris mob," overran the palace of Louis XVI and established a revolutionary government that led to the execution of Louis and the royal family, and which was followed by a decade of civil war. Here, the modern idea of "left" and "right" were developed, with those alleged to support the nobility being seated to the right in the French Parliament. As in modern times, these ideas were nonsense, because all supporters of the nobility were executed very early on in the revolution and, as honest monarchists disappeared, revolutionary "republicans" were defined further right relative to the more and more extreme factions sitting on the left. Eventually, Maximilien Robespierre, a French revolutionary who had led the execution of the French nobility, became defined as a "right winger" relative to the "left-wing" forces of the leader of the Paris mob, Jean-Paul Marat, and was executed as a counter-revolutionary.

This revolution, which was the first revolution to be characterized by the mass executions and terror which would define the similar communist and democratic revolutions of the 20th century, was defeated by the ascension of Napoleon. However, Napoleon himself was a Republican—just not one as extreme as Marat and Robespierre—and his conquest of Europe was essentially anti-aristocratic in nature, at least in its origin. As it turned more imperial, it met more resistance from powers such as Britain, which eventually knocked Napoleon off his throne. What Napoleon and the French Revolution gave Europe, though, was the idea of the "nation" independent from the aristocracy that ruled it—the idea that the people as a whole defined the state, instead of the rule of select personage. This idea, known as "bourgeois nationalism," was a major step in deracializing Europe, as its essence was that the mass of the people, and not the best of the people, were paramount. From this idea would come the nationalization and unity of Italy and Germany in the late 19th century.

These three revolutions set the stage for Europe in the 19th century, where the Jews, newly liberated by Masonic democracies and republics, would create the ideological foundation for their revolutions of the 20th century, with democratic capitalism, international socialism and Zionism being their weapons of war.

What emerges from this thumbnail sketch of Jewish history, and of the history of democratic and communist revolution in general, is a group of people, with their gentile allies, who see themselves as the paramount outsiders and who are waging a desperate war to destroy civilization, and reduce the beauty of ordered white, Western or European society into hateful, destructive chaos. Beginning in Egypt, where they saw themselves as the descendents of the wilderness god Seth, the Jews have defined themselves in opposition to Indo-European or Aryan society, while simultaneously profiting by siphoning off the wealth of that society.

As the Jews developed, they associated their god with the serpent-demon Typhon, whose sole function in Greek myth was as a rebel against the Aryan Zeus and his fellow gods. When the Roman empire became ascendant, the Jews simultaneously entered the Roman court and agitated rebellion against the Roman government, seeking to profit from both Rome's growth and its destruction. This pattern would define the Jewish relationship to white society for the remainder of their history.

To contextualize the role of the Jews, an analogy to Indo-European myth may be in order. In the Vedas, as in the Zend-Avesta and the Nordic Eddas, there is a race of smiths, the Ribhus, who are not gods—they are, in fact, beings of a much more common and less exalted type—who work with the gods to fashion the great things of the universe. But these Ribhus revolt against the gods and turn against divine society, and in the struggle of these underworld smith and the divine might of the Aryan people comes the disintegration and dismantling of the orderly world—and the spreading of the chaos of the wilderness—which culminates in the destruction of mankind and life on Earth. In the Eddas, these angry smiths forge a magic sword, the mis-named "Sword of Victory," which they wield against the Hammer of Thor with success, routing the gods and spreading winter, until the day of Ragnarok, when the two sides find mutual destruction and the light-bringing demon Surt destroys the Earth with fire.

Are the ribhus the Jews' rabbis? Expelled as an unwanted and criminal underclass from Aryan society in the dawn of prehistory, the Jews have defined history as a conflict between them and their "sword of victory," the three-headed giant of internationalism, and the national and social feelings of the traditional Aryan peoples. With the lion of international capitalism, the serpent of international communism and the goat of international Zionism, the Jews are a chimera seeking to devour healthy Indo-European society. Breathing the fire of "democracy" from all three of its heads, it wages war upon a world it has blinded to its demonic nature.

As we will see, this attack, and the strategy of disinformation and illusion which has covered it, was almost a century in the womb before it was unleashed full scale upon the West.

ENDNOTE:

1 The transliteration of Indo-European proper names into Semitic script is best illustrated in Hittite literature. Semitic scripts generally use a vowel-consonant, consonant-vowel, or vowel structure in their syllabic alphabets. Indo-European names transliterated into such tend to take the extra letter and not pronounce it. Thus "IOVE" would become "Ja-Ho-Ov-Ah" or "Yahweh." The argument that Iove is related to the proto-Indo-European root *Diw is almost certainly incorrect, as *Diw has a vowel and semi-vowel sound which transform into a form like *Zeu-, *Tiw- and *Iu-, and not the vowel-vowel-semi-vowel of Iov-. Iov- is very likely a word of Etruscan or early Minoan origin, and related to the Etruscan Great Mother goddess Iuno.

CHAPTER TWO

THE BEGINNING
OF THE END OF NORMAL

As was outlined in the introduction, there existed in the Indo-European world from the greatest of antiquity a state of "normality" that, while it has been in decay since almost its conception, had maintained generally stable forms along the almost the entirety of the 6,000 years of relatively well-known world history, despite the efforts of an undercurrent of essentially religious hatred, linked to ideas of chaos, the wilderness and evil, which had spent these millennia gnawing at its roots like the dragon at the tree of life. The seeds of what was to come can be traced back to the Middle Ages, to Roman decadence, even into the Middle Kingdom of Egypt and beyond, but it was the Reformation in Europe which set the stage for the decadence of the modern era. The Reformation let loose a sea of anti-Catholic but Christian forces that were co-opted by demonic movements and the Jews, and which were turned into a series of political revolutions that established in power the movements that sowed the seeds of the larger inversion of the normal that characterized the 19th and 20th centuries.

The first head of this monster, the chimera of Jewish power, is democracy, which we see established in the Glorious Revolution in England and the American Revolution in the American colonies. The second head of the monster is communism, and we have discussed how the French Revolution was a proto-Bolshevik movement which developed using the rhetoric of democracy, but with the motives of hatred for any social division that acknowledges the moral or spiritual superiority of one segment over another. The third head of the chimera is Zionism, the desire for a Jewish state—a base of operations from which the crime syndicate can operate—which grew parallel to and in accordance with the movements that the revolutionaries of the post-Reformation, Renaissance and Enlightenment eras unleashed upon the world.

In the opening years of the 19th century, Napoleon suppressed the French Revolution, leading his forces as the "savior of parliament," but seizing power and establishing the French empire, which was essentially revolutionary and republican in nature. He marched across Europe, toward even Moscow, in an effort to spread the republican-imperial banner, and he is stopped by the Russian winter and the British military, who are themselves intent upon expanding their empire. In both the British and French governments of this period we see the parallel influences of Freemasonry and Judaism, Freemasonry, as was illustrated, being an extension of the worship of Baal which developed in the Middle Ages in response to the pseudo-scholarly doctrines of the Catholic Church, themselves derived from a half-learned idea of history and of Roman polemicizing against their perennial enemies in the Persian empire.

The importance of Napoleon and his defining role in the 19th century cannot be overestimated. His two greatest acts of destruction were the annihilation of two empires—the Holy Roman and the Spanish—and the creation of a power void in

Europe and the Americas into which the forces of democracy and the young communist movement stepped. Yet Napoleon was not an unequivocally destructive figure. Much less radical than the French revolutionaries he suppressed, he was also an opponent of the international banking families which had begun to emerge in Europe, particularly the Rothschild family, which was allied with the Hesse-Kassel line of European nobility, an opponent of Napoleon, and the Hapsburgs, who were eventually persuaded to join the alliance of Germany and Russia against the Napoleonic forces. This opposition to the international bankers who had, already, at this period gained control of the bank of England is what eventually led to Napoleon's demise, as well as to the ascendency of the Rothschilds, who stepped into the void created by the smashing of the temporal power of their gentile hosts.

The suppression of Napoleon allowed the ascendency of the British empire, and the dismantling of the French empire ended one of the prime counterbalances to and opponents of British power. Indeed, by the end of the century, France had become so irrelevant in its real power that the traditional enemy of Britain could be seen as a bit of a lesser ally and trusted sidekick, as Britain became to the United States in the 20th century. Napoleon's defeat also saved the monarchies of Europe—but, in doing so, unleashed a force, what Julius Evola would later refer to as "bourgeois nationalism," which further pushed Europe forward into abnormality and degradation.

Traditionally, a people defines itself by race or ethnicity. In Europe, before the 19th century, there was the German people, who enjoyed a fundamental unity, even though, politically, they were shattered into several dozen petty states. Similarly, there was an Italian people, trapped in the same fragmented politics, but conscious of their identity as Italians. Even in France, there were strong ethnic associations, remnants of the time when France was a series of warring kingdoms, even if all of these ethnicities were governed over by the same crown. This idea of essential unity despite political division was in many ways a remnant of the feudal system, in which a local ruler governed over whatever lands and towns and castles he had the force to possess, struggling against other local rulers, all of whom might nominally owe allegiance to the same crown or the same king. There could be political divisions, but the political divisions did not define the people.

In contrast, the petty nationalism promoted by the Napoleonic movement in Europe was a prototype of the kind of confused nationalism that defines the modern nation state. Instead of there being Gascons and Bretons and Normans and others, there were only the French people—the undifferentiated mob of Paris, consisting of the worst elements of the human race in France, so debased and degraded that even the things which should have differentiated them were so cheapened as to be nothing. Similarly, in what was once the Holy Roman Empire, the idea emerged that instead of there being German peoples owing allegiance to Bavaria or Prussia or Austria or the other crowns and petty nobles, there was a Germany, within whose borders there were only German people, and outside of whom there were people who were not German. Thus, the absurdity of the musical *The Sound of Music*, wherein a member of the Austrian nobility asserts he is not German, or the absurdity of the Jewish argument against Hitler—that he was "Austrian" rather than "German" because of an accident of the political borders at his birth. The idea that the limits of political authority define the social collective is the first major 19th century irrationality that destroyed Europe.

Oswald Spengler, in his *Decline of the West*, talks of the many points of light that brightened the surface of the Earth as the great cultures of antiquity were brought into being. Similarly, he describes the cultural whole as a type of biological origin, a collective in which each individual being plays a specialized and differentiated, but harmonious, role. These socio-cultural organisms are biological and spiritual in nature, and are broadly divided among men in race and ethnicity. Despite what political borders may exist, all people who partake of the socio-cultural whole are one.

The petty-national idea of the 19th century is that which in the 20th century says that all the humans within the boundaries of the United States of America are American, even if one is Negro, another mestizo and a third of German or Irish origin. At the time of its development, when all of those within the borders of France were essentially French, even if some were admixed in a greater or lesser degree with the Nordic, south Germanic, Anglo-Saxon or Celtic racial type, the petty nationalism of the 19th century was hard to distinguish from an authentic nationalism. Many authentic nationalists, in fact, embraced it. But the idea that the limits of the authority of the state define the limits of the racial-collective soul of the people is an absurdity that the only the Jews, with their deeply artificial social and political systems, could embrace.

With Republicanism and this nationalism, though, came the integration of the Jew, and the release of the Jew from his ghetto across the whole of Europe. After all, if the Jew is within the borders governed by the nation, then he too, like all of the other peoples of the nation, is a citizen, entitled to "equal rights" and an equal station within the society. He can cast his vote, earn his money, spend his money, own his property, and if he never abandons his own internal idea of race, he can at least speak in flowing words and pretend to embrace the willful annihilation that is eliminating the land of the racial instincts which could oppose him. Thus, in the beginning of the 19th century, one sees the Jew, who has already established himself as the secret backer of the anti-Catholic and Protestant movements that granted him admission to the nation that allowed him to create the banking institutions with which he would come to rule the world, being culturally liberated, leaving the ghettos, and assuming a prominent role in the discourse of the nations.

Thus the 19th century sees the seeds of the intellectualisms which would dominate the 20th century creeping, like the Jew, out of the ghettoes, and planting themselves like poisonous weeds in the heart of European learning. These academic and intellectual movements were: in economics and politics, that of Marx and his successors; in psychology, Sigmund Freud; in anthropology and racial science, Franz Boas; and in sociology, the "Frankfurt School." Of these, Marx and his comrade Engels are the first that should be examined, because Marxism was the first of these movements and the trunk from which the others branched off, and was a unique product of the Jewish urge toward destruction wrapped in the language of studied ignorance.

In the traditional Aryan view of the world, movement forward in time is a struggle between the god of Order and the forces of Chaos, the latter being manifest, in the Vedic tradition, in the form of the death god Mahakala, the Great Destroyer, who is nothing but time himself. In the Eddas, even Thor struggles against, and cannot defeat, time, and all of the Aryan religions saw time as the essential core and driving force of social decay. In the beginning, there are the castes, and the system of social order which is based upon the castes and the differentiation of social function. As the forces of chaos grow in power, society breaks down, and with it, social and racial differentiation. This inability of human beings to find a place to be in which matches their inherent nature is the root of discontent—each human being has a place which is different from that of others and most like others of their type, and when society refuses to provide differentiated roles and, instead, forces all human beings into the same role, or refuses to guide some human beings into their appropriate role, instead giving them "choices" which they are constitutionally unable to handle, society itself becomes progressively less able to function and breaks down.

From this idea of the degeneration of the castes—the systematic breakdown of society so that the gods are replaced by the priests, who are replaced by the warriors, who are replaced by the merchants, who are replaced by the slaves—Marx created the idea of the succession of the classes, essentially a plagiarism of traditional Aryan religion inverted in principle so that what is, in Indo-European society, evil, in the Marxist-Jewish society becomes good. Marx hung his hat on the German philosopher Hegel, who paraphrased this notion of progressive breakdown of ideas in terms of the progress of human society, by stating that each thing is a thesis which creates, through its action, an anti-thesis, and through interaction with its antithesis creates a new thesis, or synthesis, that is more advanced than the one which preceded it. In a sense, Hegel's ideology was an extension of that of Aristotle, who saw virtue in the mean between two extremes, but it was also a justification of the march forward of time, which Hegel was unable to see as the force which not only brings all things into being, but which also destroys them and renders them into nothingness.

Thus Marx took the warrior caste which was manifest in the European aristocracy, and posited their opposition to the merchant class of the European bourgeoisies—the class which, with the aid of Marx's co-religionists and in service to the Baal-ic cults of Freemasonry, has recently established themselves in republican and parliamentary revolutions across the continent. Marx predicted, correctly, that these revolutions would spur a greater movement for "liberation" that would end in the bourgeoisie being supplanted by "the workers"—and, really, by the lowest, non-working, criminal and sub-human elements of the "workers," whose only claim to being "working class" was the fact that they did not own capital. In traditional Aryan society, this "revolt of the slaves" was a prelude to Ragnarok; in Marxist rhetoric, it was a prelude to the "end of history." One should recognize that the two events are the same. Marx intended to bring the human race to an apocalypse.

Marx's emergence gave rise to the spirit of revolution which has plagued Europe, the West, and the world ever since, and which reached its latest peak in the United States with the election of the mulatto Marxist, Barack Obama. His method was one that Jews of all political stripes would employ over the next two centuries: he sought to find divisions in society, and then to exploit those divisions so that the two sides, instead of working harmoniously for a common social goal, fought each other in a mutually self-destructive fashion that only benefited the outsiders to the conflict: the Jews.

As Marx and his adherents in the communist and socialist movements of Europe goaded on the workers, other Jews, banking Jews and Jews who had infiltrated the upper classes, goaded on the aristocracy and the mercantile bourgeois against the workers. While the majority of Jews always sided with the revolutionary movements, a minority of Jews always sided against them, and the two played off each other by appearing to work against each other, while really working in tandem to exploit and exacerbate social tensions, all the while controlling the "dialogue" by assuming the leadership of both sides, and waging no real struggle against each other—just against the people their mis-leadership was destroying.

These tactics were at the root of the worker's uprisings which grasped Europe in the mid-19th century, particularly the 1848 revolutions in Germany and across Europe, which were a product of the Marxists and the chaos that followed the efforts to re-establish monarchies in the nations which had been de-stroyed during the Napoleonic Wars. In nations that had been left leaderless—such as the former states of the Holy Roman Empire—parliamentary movements and efforts at a unity gov-ernment based upon a confederacy of nations emerged. In Ger-many in particular, Austria and Prussia became the major contestants in the effort to establish spheres of influence and to fill the power void that had been left by the dis-establishment of the empire. But the revolutions of 1848 were not limited to the southern German nations—they occurred across Europe, and involved petty nationalist movements in France, Hungary, Denmark, Spain and other nations. In many areas, these "lib-eral" democratic and communist movements—led by Jews—were able to gain concessions, such as the establishment of parliaments and the end of autocratic rule. In others, they were suppressed by the traditional forces of Europe.

On the back of these aborted attempts to seize control of the central and eastern European states, the Jews in the commu-nist movement established the Communist Internationale, which was to struggle "for working people," i.e., for Jewish in-terests, across the European continent and the world. The first principle of this communist movement (and its anarchist and socialist and social-democratic tendrils) was that it was to be international in scope—it would recognize no borders—as the Jews were an international people and the national borders only indicated the limits of the temporal power of their ene-mies. From the beginning, the Jews were not content to rule only one segment of the earth, but all of it—and the Commu-nist Internationale made that goal explicit.

Similarly, while the worker's revolution was busily promot-ing internationalism and the international unity of the working class, a similar movement among the banking Jews and the elite was greedily promoting the internationalist nature of capital—

particularly in the context of the capitalist Jews' greatest ally, the British empire. The empire had entered its Victorian period, which was a period of its greatest expansion and power, and had developed such an international scope that it truly could be said that the Sun never set upon it. Though it had lost its American colonies to an early Jewish-Masonic social experiment in managed chaos, its essential function was to promote the Jewish goal of world unity through its introduction of the "European" culture the Jews were creating into what is today called the Third World. The dark peoples of the world had existed outside of history for much of humanity's reign on the planet. Having achieved nothing and built nothing, they had no role to play in international affairs. But the Jews sought everywhere for recruits to lead in their army, and sought to steal from everyone and every living thing that could be stolen from. As essentially a death movement, they sought to kill all life, and the fact that any portion of the world's living beings would stay outside their reign was abhorrent to them. So they drove their capitalist machine forward and conquered, filling the heads of whites with phony (as opposed to valid) notions about race and nation, and developing an international system in the Western world, already prepared for the Jews by democracy, while taking a different tack in central and eastern Europe.

The British economic system has generally been described as mercantilist, in which the raw materials of the subject peoples in the colonies were brought to the homeland for processing into manufactured goods, which were then sold on the international market, including back to the colonies from which the raw materials were taken, and this system is generally correct. The Jews wanted to rule the world, but they did not physically wish to trek through jungles and swelter in the heat of the desert to do so—they reclined in the luxuries of London, directing the trade that fattened their pockets, but not physically going out in their pith helmets and attempting to subjugate the darkies. Thus the Jews used the international aspect of the British empire to develop a system that allowed for international trade to be directed from a centralized location—a tactic they would build upon over the next two centuries.

The British Jews also expanded their influence into America, where the London banking houses, already dominated by Jewish families such as the Rothschilds, who had come to prominence during the Napoleonic Wars, established alliances with American banking houses, such as the Morgans, providing the capital that fueled the industrial revolution. While America had been a successful development in the international democratic revolution of the 18th century, by being first, it had set itself outside the international system the Jews were forging to rule the world, and a signature aspect of this was its economic independence. Having been founded on a revolution nominally against taxation, the American people were opposed to efforts to centralize their economy, and money flowed freely, allowing the establishment of local economic powers that were largely independent of the international system.

This development—the development of what the Marxists term the petty bourgeoisie—is what truly infuriates the Jew, much more than any injustice created by his centralized system of power. When an individual breaks free from the Jewish system and begins to develop wealth independent of that system, the Jew invariably labels that individual "corrupt" and begins to agitate against him as an example of the alleged evils of the system that produced him. Thus, in America of the 19th century, images of "fat-cat" politicians and businessmen—always gentile—were developed in the Jewish press and agitated by the Jews among the American workers. But, even when the wealth of such people is acquired by corrupt means—and, often, it is the product of hard work and sharp business skills, not corruption—the Jew attacks them not because they are not corrupt, but because they are not Jewish and in vassalage to international Judaism. This applies on the local scale, when a businessman is not in line with the Jewish system, and on the national scale, when a nation breaks free from the Jewish system. What begins as noise ends in violence—either legal action, which is itself violence regulated by "society," or war.

Thus the Jews inflicted upon America the so-called Civil War, whose primary goal was to destroy the independent wealth of the post-feudal aristocracy of the American South, in favor of the Northern aristocracy, which had largely allied itself with the Jewish-dominated British banking elite. Slavery was the system that America had chosen out of necessity to control the animalistic and unmanageable Negro underclass that the monarchs of Europe had imposed upon the continent. The original settlers of the Americas, back to the 16th century, had not wanted the Negro in their settlements. As early as the first decade of that century, Spanish colonists in the Caribbean were writing letters to the king of Spain, demanding that the Negroes he was forcing upon their colonies be returned to Africa. But the king was largely detached from the sufferings of the people, and he wanted slave labor to work his plantations—labor the American natives were largely unsuited for. So the Negro was forced upon the settlers of the Americas, and the settlers of the Americas were forced to adopt the only social system that allowed for social control of this unsocial and uncontrollable element—slavery.

Beginning with the Jewish and Masonic agitations of the 18th century, though, an anti-slavery movement had developed in the American colonies led by a combination of radical Christians, Masonic libertarians, and the communist rabble of the Paris Mob. This movement coincided with the general independence of the French and Spanish colonies of the Americas which followed the Napoleonic Wars. These movements varied in the degree of their radicalism, but all were fueled by racial and ideological animosities that were largely irrational and part of the general chthonic movement of the times. The French Revolution essentially left the French colonies in the Americas adrift, and, in Haiti, where the small white population was vastly outnumbered by the blacks, the agitators of the Mob incited the Negroes and mulattos to overthrow the French elite, massacring the whites, and then inciting the Negroes to overthrow the mulatto elite that replaced them, also with a general massacre. The result was the transformation of the western portion of Hispaniola into an African state—complete with cannibalism, voodoo and the general degradation and mockery of life which is the way of the Negro people.

Parallel to these revolutions were the revolts that occurred in the nations of the Americas in the early part of the 19th centuries—the Bolivarist revolutions—that led to the independence of the Spanish colonies. With its engagement and eventual defeat by France in the Napoleonic wars, the Spanish crown was no longer able to maintain its authority in its colonies, and the new American government, which was essentially anti-European in its perspective, wished to end European involvement in American colonies and establish an American (USA) sphere. Thus the Spanish elite of the colonies, often under the guise of a movement of the people, led movements which shaved their colonies off of their motherland and created independent "nations" in the Masonic-democratic model, often with a racial aspect, generated by the interbreeding of the white Latino elite with the indigenous peoples of the Americas as well. In much of South America, where the population of the core areas was overwhelmingly white, or where strict systems of slavery existed and the indigenous peoples outside the whites' control were separated by geographical factors—jungles and mountains—

these revolutions went relatively smoothly. In nations such as Mexico, which became a battleground for proxy wars between the French and the Spanish, they developed into dangerous anti-social movements.

Simon Bolivar himself was allied with the Masonic forces, and received aid from Negro and mulatto soldiers from Haiti, when he began his revolt against Spanish rule in what is now Venezuela. In Mexico, his counterpart was the devil-worshipping priest Padre Miguel Hidalgo, who is still seen as an icon of revolution in that country. Across the former Spanish empire, French Masonic forces instigated anti-Spanish and anti-Hapsburg revolutions (as the Hapsburgs had taken the Spanish throne), while the American government, also Masonic in nature, waged war to conquer the northern Mexican territories. The United States encouraged Texan and Californian independence and eventually invading Mexico during the Mexican War.

On the backdrop of these revolutions, the American people had been steadily expanding to the west, exploiting the chaos caused by the wars involving France and Spain to snatch up their colonies and territorial claims, purchasing Louisiana and Florida and waging a brief war against Mexico and two against Britain in its efforts to maintain independence and push its borders to the Pacific Ocean. But the problem existed of an aristocracy in the Americas that was largely independent of the Jewish systems. Jewish "working-class" agitation had no meaning in a society that was largely based upon and approved of chattel slavery— Negro slaves could hardly agitate for their "rights," because society did not recognize they had any. Further, the "poor white trash" of the South similarly owed its origins to bonded labor, and the idea that the Southern white worker had rights vis-à-vis the plantation owner was alien to the Southern culture. Further, the elite of the South, largely Scotch-Irish in origin, had found a national identity in their common persecution by the Jewish-

British system which had been embraced by the Northern party of the United States, and thus would not voluntarily integrate into an international banking system operated from London by world Jewry.

This conflict between the largely independent American Masonic forces and the centralizing efforts that the Jews and the Rothschild family had focused upon London and the British empire first manifested themselves in the War of 1812, which began after the American Congress rejected a British effort, directed by the Rothschilds, to establish an American central bank, dependent on the Bank of London, and refused to renew charters for Rothschild interests in the United States. The Rothschilds, at the time, promised Congress in open session that they would seek vengeance through war, and war is what America got, with Britain invading America and, at one point, burning the White House.

As the decades progressed, Britain used its power and the English ethnic background of the American Yankee North to develop ties with the ruling families—what became the "Eastern Establishment"—but found the American South much less inclined to fall in line with its program for world control. The British and the international forces behind them believed that the South had to be forced into the American idea of "nationhood," in which any inhabitant within a given political border is a member of the "people," and its slaves and bonded laborers had to be made into "citizens," given a right to vote they were unprepared for and made "equals" with a culture-bearing stratum that they could never aspire to participate in. In furtherance of this, agitation on the racial question was substituted for agitation on the question of "workers' rights"—the one being too advanced, the more primitive method was chosen. Thus the Jews, who had allied with and often guided the Masonic societies which had developed from Scotch-Irish national idea of independence that, in part, established the American Revolution—turned upon their former allies as a discarded and more primitive form of the world-destroying principle, and consumed them.

The agitation began with Christian-Protestant propaganda in the churches of the Northern states. The Catholic Church had been, historically, the force in Europe that had struggled the hardest for racial equality—Dominican friars had begun agitation on the question as early as the 15th century, soon after the discovery of the Americas. But, in the United States, proto-New-Age Christian movements in the North became the leading advocates of abolition. In many cases, these groups were led by those same Freemasons who had conducted their agitation against the monarchy under the guise of religious conscious in the 17th and 18th centuries. There is nothing in the Christian religion that necessitated these people's opposition to the Southern system of slavery—slavery and feudal bondage had been a norm in most Christian countries of various stripes throughout most of Christianity's history. Their motives appear to have been a mix of ideological and ethnic, with their largely English antecedents, now allied with the Jews, being hostile to the largely Scotch-Irish aristocracy of the South, and their hatred of all notions of any man elevating himself above the lowest elements of humanity.

Regardless of their motives, these organizations linked themselves to their sister groups within the British empire, which waged an international war on the slave trade and upon slavery. In part, this was a war on the other ruling families of Europe, particularly the Hapsburgs, who had established the new dynasty of the Spanish monarchy, which had played a leading role in the trade. In part, it was a continuation of the Masonic spirit. But the slave nations of the time were universally Britain's enemies, and the attack on the slave trade was a continuation of the war the British, with their Jewish backers, were waging for international economic and political control.

The Masons had used the "Christian" feelings of the Protestants in Europe to attack and destroy the continent's Catholic monarchies, and a similar tactic was used in the United States to attack and destroy the Southern aristocracy. America became a "Christian" nation—in context, the phrase also had racial implications throughout much of the 18th and into the 19th centuries, but the "Christianization" of the Negroes had forced the use of the term "white" throughout the South (white people, at the time, being largely ignorant of their Aryan and Indo-European heritage). And, in the "Christian" foundation of the nation came a spirit to make all people equal before God by destroying those systems that made man un-equal. Not for the last time, Christianity would be harnessed in the service of communism.

In the run-up to the Civil War, the United States was badly divided by regional political parties, the majority of which advocated slavery, simply to different degrees. As the pro-slavery movement was splintered among different warring factions, a minority—the radical, anti-slavery Republicans—were able to seize the election by winning a plurality for their candidate, Lincoln, who was not as radical as they had hoped, but radical enough to destroy the South in a fratricidal war.

The Civil War was fought, and, eventually, it was won by the North. Jews certainly participated in the Southern government—taking control of the reins of trade and of the production of war materials, they made sure that a shortage of everything from basic foodstuffs to iron nails occurred throughout the Confederate States, and they profited by it, selling all they could steal from the government back to the people at exorbitant rates. Again, the methods of Joseph in Egypt were applied. And, at the end, as the restoration of peace allowed their president, Lincoln, to begin seriously contemplating the repatriation of Southern blacks to Africa, a Jewish actor, John Wilkes Booth, assassinated him. Booth himself reportedly hated the fact he had Jewish roots.

Thus the racial struggle, which would define much of American politics to the present day, was born, and it became the vehicle by which the Marxists of the 19th century imported class struggle into the United States. Lacking an aristocracy to agitate against, the Jews would agitate against the white majority, finding that the instruments of propaganda which would open the 20th century were, in fact, adequate to make a large portion of a people hate themselves.

Following the destruction of the Southern aristocracy in the United States, the Jewish-British-Masonic forces had firmly established their control over the Americas, as their parallel revolutions in the Central and South American colonies had quickly swept away the vestiges of Spanish rule and created petty-"national" movements that embraced Masonic principles and were firmly within the sphere of the world democratic revolution. In Europe, they had destroyed the Spanish empire and the Holy Roman Empire, but they had not successfully expanded their influence into the east. The monarchies of Prussia, Austria and Russia remained, and the Prussian empire in particular was rapidly expanding its influence west, into the territories that had been "liberated" from empire during the Napoleonic wars.

In the south of Europe, Italy was brought into the petty-nationalist sphere during the Risorgimento, which was the movement of national unity which destroyed the Austrian Hapsburgs' Kingdom of the Two Sicilies and established in power a king and parliament who were firmly allied to the growing international banking system and the world-destroying movement. However, in northern and central Europe, Prussia and Austria warred with each other through proxy in an effort to control the southern and western German states (Prussia having already absorbed almost all of eastern Germany), and Prussia emerged victorious. The result of this was the establishment of the Second Reich, largely, but not totally, independent of the world-destroying movement, but with some vestiges of democracy, including a token parliament that remained a paper tiger during the reign of Bismarck. Socialism and liberalism had little power under the Prussian aristocracy, and Prussia established itself as a counterpoint in northern and central Europe to British efforts to establish world economic control.

In Russia, the aristocracy was the most intransigent in its resistance to the forces that had seized control of western Europe, and it was here that the Jews and their communist movements adopted the most radical tactics, conducting bombings and assassinations and seeking the violent overthrow of the czar and his family. Yet Russia remained too powerful for a handful of Jewish agitators to overcome, and the unwillingness of its monarchy to "compromise" with the forces that sought to destroy it caused it to become a focus of Jewish anger. Recognizing the essentially racial nature of the threat against it, Russia conducted a number of pogroms during this period, expelling its Jews, often into Germany, where the Russian Jews established themselves as an underclass when compared with their "liberated" German-Jewish counterparts, and laid the foundation of the racial problems that would explode in central Europe in the 20th century.

The destruction of traditional centers of authority that had followed the victories of the Masonic and democratic movements and the wars of Napoleon had led to the liberation of Jews from their ghettoes and from restrictions on their economic and intellectual activity across Europe, and by the end of the century, these newly liberated Jews, and not just the radicals of the infant communist movement, began to wage their war from inside, as well as outside, the traditional European establishment. The end of the 19th century saw the ascension of Jews to power within the universities, where they established a number of intellectual movements that would blossom into full-blown culture-poison in the early 20th century.

First, there was the economic-intellectual movement of Marxism, which posed as a critique of the centralization of wealth in the hands of the traditional European elite, while seeking, as a solution, the centralization of wealth in the hands of a workers' state that would be controlled and guided by Jews. Under the guise of economic critique, the Marxist movement sought to exacerbate the natural social division between worker and governor to increase Jewish power, and this intellectual-university version of Marxism would evolve into the social democratic movement which controls Europe and the United States today.

In anthropology there was the movement of Boas, which sought to break down theories of racial and caste differentiation by advocating the claim that all men were equal, and the most primitive of human societies were essentially proto-versions of the most advanced. In this model, the black Africans with their mud huts were simply humans, like whites and Asians and other peoples, but who had lacked the opportunity for advancement due to environmental factors or systematic oppression, and represented human society in its earliest forms—societies from which the more advanced civilizations could learn. This movement derived from the ideas of the origins of man which were postulated during the French Revolution, and which have no basis in fact or observed history. No black African society has ever modernized itself or developed a civilization or culture without being propped up and controlled by whites or another more advanced people, and none of the primitives sought by Boas and his Jewish school of anthropology had anything to contribute to the understanding of the traditional roots of Indo-European society. Yet, in conjunction with the spirit of the times, this worship of primitivism was able to impose itself upon the sound racial science of the European, and to establish itself as the norm during the 20th century.

In psychology came, in the early 20th century, the doctrines of Sigmund Freud, which parallel the movements of Boas and Marx in the personal spheres. Freud was a cocaine addict who invented his theories as he went along, but, as with many Jews, he was blessed with the gift of words, and was able to persuade much of the white world that their troubles originated in sexual inadequacies and thoughts about the anus, while reinterpreting much of the Indo-European mythical tradition in terms of base sexual urges, frustrated or understood "collectively." Freud's parallel in the sphere of physics would be Einstein, who stole the little that his theories had of value from his Serbian wife and from gentile physicists he associated with, and who was promoted as the "world's smartest man" primarily because of his Jewishness and his radical communist politics, not because of the quality of his thought.

Perhaps the most important movement that emerged from the late 19th century, in terms of its impact on the world and its furtherance of the destruction of human society, was Zionism, which was the Jewish adoption of the ideals of petty nationalism combined with a militant desire to destroy the world. For much of the early 20th century, Zionism and communism would battle for the support of the Jewish people, who, as they emerged as world controllers, disputed among themselves how best to mislead and destroy the gentile peoples over whom they would rule.

The Zionist movement began in the same "liberated" areas of southern Germany that would see the communist 1848 revolutions, and quickly spread and found support in the United

States, Britain and among Jews across the world. Holding regular meetings from 1845 onward, "reformed" Jews who had integrated the liberal idea of national revolution and the intellectual movements that derived from Marxism began to agitate among the Western democracies for the establishment of a Jewish state. Where this state would be and what would be its nature remained a subject of intense debate, and there were several nascent colonialist movements that involved Jewish migration to spots from the Mississippi Valley in the American South to the island of Madagascar.

From this Zionist movement, however, developed a political consciousness and a political movement among Jews that became more explicit in its world-destroying aims as it developed from a radical religious-nationalist views into a world-controlling conspiracy. The "Elders of Zion"—the council of rabbis which controlled the Zionist movement in the 19th century—were a real body of Jewish thinkers who, by the late 1890s and the founding of the World Zionist Organization, had won the support of Jewish bankers and other prominent Jews, as well as a position of power and respectability in the world Jewish movement.

The aims and intentions of these Elders of Zion are best captured in their Protocols, which has often been attacked by Jewish organizations as a forgery, not because it is fundamentally untrue in its description of the efforts of world Jewry, but because it is, allegedly, an imperfect copy of the original notes of a conference of Zionist rabbis which had occurred shortly before its publication. As the thinker Julius Evola has noted, whether or not the Protocols of the Elders of Zion is literally true is less important than the fact that it is spiritually true and an accurate depiction of what the Jews were doing and actually did in the sphere of world politics during the 20th century.

The Protocols begin with the assertion that the Jews must

rule the world by force, and that, in the modern world, money is the means by which force can be purchased. The Jews are to seek control of the press and to use class divisions in modern society to wage economic war on powers and nations which resist their aim of world control. The serpent is the emblem of the Jewish people because it represents resistance to Christianity and gentile religion, and Freemasonry and the rule of "reason" are to act as a proxy for the Jews—an irony, as it was the Freemasonic movement which won the Jews their liberation from the ghettoes. The republic and the capitalist system are to the be the first stages of Jewish rule, as they are the form of government and economy which the gentile mercantile elite desire. Once established, the Jews are to infiltrate the republican forms of government and manipulate parliamentary systems using their financial power to create great centralization of the state. By controlling monopolies, the Jews can spread poverty, and then promote a culture of escapism from that poverty, in the form of anarchist theories, sexual liberation, and the promotion of drunkenness and drug abuse. Simultaneously, the Jews will promote international conflict and instigate wars between the states they control, using these wars to kill the best elements of the populations they control and to weaken those nation states until they are unable to resist Jewish rule. All the while, the Jews are to infiltrate the offices of government, particularly the judiciary, while aligning their political faction with the mob and the lowest elements of humanity, who will be manipulated to use political violence to suppress all forms of dissent.

As the Jews gain control over individual nations, these nations are to be united in an international body—what became, in the 20th century, the League of Nations, and then the United Nations—which will begin to take authority away from its individual nation states, until a single "lord of all the world" is to be declared. An international constitution, using the rhetoric of international freedom and equality, while, in actuality, enslaving the non-Jewish peoples of the world, is to be established. The people are to be distracted by the press and appropriate entertainment provided while their actual standard of living decreases. A new religion is to be created to provide succor to the people, and pornography, prostitution and drugs are to be further promoted to provide escapes from the meaninglessness of the Jewish-Masonic world. Eventually, the Masons are to be pushed aside, and the Jews are to rule independently and directly as the "chosen" people. Universities are to be tightly controlled, and are to serve as a mechanism for the control of ideas within society. The new religion is to embrace the Jews as the founders of Christianity, and to hold them more holy than Christ. Today John Hagee says the same thing.

To control this society, a secret police force consisting of the entire population is to be mobilized. Directed by the central control, the people are to be encouraged to spy on and report each other, as they live in constant fear of conspiracies that either do not exist, or exist solely as creations of the Jewish central authority. Rights against arrest are to be abrogated, and Jewish control of the judiciary will prevent any deviation in the use of those arrested for propaganda purposes. Sedition and political crimes are to become the paramount concern of the state, while common crime is only mildly punished, if it is to be punished at all.

Taxes are to be used to appropriate the wealth of the people and centralize it in the hands of the Jews. An international system of debt is to be created to guarantee the payment of interest to the international Jewish banks. As wealth becomes concentrated in the hands of the Jews, parallel with their political power, all old forms of society are to be completely destroyed as the Jews transition to massive slave states, in which the gentile people work solely for the benefit of the Jews, and retain none of the products of their labor. In the end, the "lord of all the world" established under the United Nations is to be re-placed by a "king of the Jews" descended from the line of David, who will then rule the world until the end of time.

This approach to world control, which contrasts only in its details with the efforts of the world communist movement, was the product of the Zionist movement, which sought to first es-tablish a national territory from which it could operate its in-ternational criminal enterprises with impunity. This world criminal base would become the nation of "Israel," established by the slaughter of Palestinians in 1948—but that invasion was the product of a century of agitation and of deep planning of the methods and means by which the Jews could establish their empire upon the Earth.

Thus, as the 19th century ended, the destructive movements which had their roots in the English, American and French dem-ocratic movements, and which spread over Europe under the empire of Napoleon, had matured into petty-bourgeois nation-alist movements which controlled all of western Europe and the Americas, and which were attempting to expand in their next form—communism—into the states of central and eastern Eu-rope. The world Zionist movement had established an alterna-tive theory of world control, based upon exploitation of the existing Masonic architecture which the Jews had established in the "democratic" states, and the dialogue and debate between world Zionism and communism set the foundations for the "democratic socialist" movement, which would eventually de-feat both and gain control of nearly the entirety of the world in the 21st century. Yet these movements had not yet fully blos-somed, and much of Europe remained intact, under Prussian, Austrian or Russian control, as the 19th century came to an end. The American South, conquered mid-century, had seen a resur-gence, and Jewish criticisms of racialist theory and European sci-ence were in their infancy.

What the Jews lacked at this time was the total control of the press and means of information which they needed to achieve their goals, as well as the tools of mass propaganda which would allow Jewish voices to eclipse gentile voices during the 20th century, until the invention of the internet and the freedom of communication which would pose the greatest challenge to continued Jewish rule. Yet the tools for such mass propaganda were developing in the technology of radio—which would then lead to the technology of television, and an unprecedented ability to project irrationalism into European cultures.

The 19th century saw the full development of democracy and petty nationalism, and the sweeping away of the traditional structures of the Western nations—particularly America, Britain and France. It saw the development of an internationalism still controlled by gentiles, but a dangerous infiltration of Jewish ideas and radicals into that gentile society. The dismantling of normal social structures and relations in the West set the stage for the abnormal, which would come to define the societies of the 20th century. And the need for the Jews to achieve total world control, combined with the intransigence of central and eastern Europe would lead to the two world-destroying wars that would consume the last vestiges of healthy European society in their flames.

CHAPTER THREE

THE END OF NORMAL;
THE BEGINNING OF THE END

Entering the 20th century, the three heads of the Jewish chimera—the serpent of communism, the lion of democracy, and the goat of Judaism—were firmly in place and dominant in world affairs. The old way of being—the way of life that had defined European mankind for millennia—was fading, and continued only in those nations who, out of the good fortune to be "underdeveloped," had proved less fitting targets for the Jews in the early stages of their ascendency.

With the hatred of those revolutionary Jews who had financed Freemasonry and now led the communist movement, came the equal hatred of British capitalism which, under the Jew Disraeli, had defined itself in the 19th century by its desire for absolute domination of all world markets. Rather than allow any autonomous economic development or independence from the British world economic system, British pseudonationalist economics required that the British empire and the Jewish-controlled Bank of London penetrate and exploit all other peoples—not only its colonies, but the independent nations of central and eastern Europe—in order to create a one world government under its rule. This role as the central nation in what would become the New World Order would, after its attempt had destroyed Britain, be passed on to Britain's successor in world affairs and in the schemes of the Jews, the United States of America.

In the United States, communist agitation against the Masonic domination of the Eastern Establishment caused the century of revolution to open with Jewish hate violence. The 1890s had been marked in the United States with the rise of various communist and anarchist movements, and these led to the assassination of the U.S. President William McKinley by Leon Czolgosz, a Polish Jew and communist whose deeds were celebrated by an established Jewish activist caste, particularly the Jewess Emma Goldman. Goldman was an anarchist agitator most noted for laying the seeds that would sprout into the feminist and abortion rights movements, and she spoke plainly in favor of a number of anarchist acts of murder directed against political figures and the wealthy.

Parallel to this rising communist movement in the United States was the rising communist movement of Russia. An abortive coup against the czar was attempted by the Jews in 1905, leading to the expulsion of many of their number from Russia and their entry into Germany, which granted them refuge. Parallel to these political movements came a wave of organized crime that was loosely centered around communist politics, but was primarily centered around the efforts of individuals to enrich themselves through criminal activity. The most notable crime these semi-communists committed was bank robbery, and the most notable of the Russian communist bank robbers was Joseph Stalin, a native Georgian who would later seize power and become dictator of the Union of Soviet Socialist Republics.

Europe, too, was torn by continued and strengthened communist agitation, as various groups attempted to exploit class divisions to win seats in the "democratic" parliaments that had lately been established in the monarchies of central and southern Europe. These efforts at class agitation were paralleled in the United States and in the European colonies by race agitation—and the National Association for the Advancement of Colored People saw its foundation by a group of well-meaning "Christians" who, within a decade, would be replaced by a motley crew of Jewish rabbis and radicals determined to force Negro barbarism into America's white society.

While the radical "left" moved forward, the other side of Jewish power, the radical "right," was busy as well—and often working toward the same ends as their nominal opposition. In terms of the racial and colonial questions, the most important segment of this "right" wing opposition were the British elite, particularly the group of politicians and activists that centered around the *London Times* newspaper, and which were allied with the "Round Table" organizations founded by Cecil Rhodes. It was from this clique that the idea of de-colonization and the creation of the British "Commonwealth," originally the idea of expanding autonomous British dominions, developed. While the Marxist agitators of the radical "left" were pushing for Britain to "liberate" its colonies, their counterparts on the radical "right" within the ruling elite were pushing for the same goal in a different structure.

Rhodes has been the industrialist who had given the colony of Rhodesia his name and who had been a British imperialist struggling for world domination for the British empire. His theory—really, the theory which gained ground in his name—was that the colonies of the empire were not best ruled directly, but should be given nominal independence while remaining under the financial and political control of the British elite. He and the set around him stated they believed that this would allow the colonized people to feel independent without actually granting them any real independence from the British system. In a sense, this has become the mantra of the gentile portion of the world elite. However, while it is a nominally different philosophy from that proposed by the radical "left," it leads in practice to the same policies as the leftists propose—essentially, decolonization and the creation of international organizations in the place of what was once a national-imperial state, as well as the elevation of the lesser races and the requirement that all white people maintain the public farce of "equality" on the national and racial level.

In the United States, by 1911, this clique was able to impose on America the Federal Reserve System, which began, in all essential points, as an extension of the British banking system, and which came, through the postwar Bretton Woods agreement, to supplant and replace that banking system as the center of world financial power. One of the things which had most upset the Jews about the American Revolution had been the continued independence of the United States from the international banking system. America chartered local and state banks and resisted efforts led by the Rothschild family to impose a national system. Yet, in the post-Civil War era of industrialism, with the exploitive capitalism of the Anglo-Saxon Establishment and the Eastern Elite finding no check to their culture destruction except, briefly, the Southern Ku Klux Klan, sufficient power became concentrated in a handful of industrial monopolies—and the banking monopolies which financed them—that these monopolies, many of them, like the Rockefellers and the Morgans, having extensive ties to London and the British empire, were able to impose on Congress the Federal Reserve Act—the cornerstone of what would become the massive system of debt, taxation and centralized wealth the United States still faces.

The issue with the Jews and their gentile compatriots has never been one of ideology. All ideology, right and left, exists to serve the same aim, which is the concentration of wealth and power in the hands of an elite—and, in the case of the Jews, an ethnic Jewish elite. While "right" and "left" define different approaches and different theories to justify that concentration of power, in practice the two theories differ very little from each other. When communists seize power, they use war and totalitarian methods to steal the wealth of the people and place it in their hands; when capitalists have power, they use the same violence and underhanded methods to centralize wealth in their hands. The only conflict the two had in the pre-World-War I period was which means of concentrating power—and, ultimately, concentrating power in the hands of the Jews—would be more efficient, and thus the central conflict of the 20th century was about how best to steal from the people and push aside the gentile power structure—and not between serious differences in opinion about how to govern a state in the best interests of its people.

But the 20th century opened with a few remnants of the 19th century that had to be cleaned up—and those were the remaining monarchies in Germany, Austria and Russia. It was for this purpose that the Jews and the British pushed the world into World War I, the first war of genocide that the Jews directed against the white race in an effort to permanently destroy that race's power.

The British were the most gullible in this, as their elite had been the most thoroughly infiltrated and dominated by the Jewish bankers. Perhaps it was because they were the first nation to fall to Jewish democracy that they were the nation in which the Jewish poison had had such effect. But the war aims of the British in World War I were very explicit and clear—they saw Germany as a threat to their control of the markets of central Europe, and they intended to remove the German monarchy in order to establish a British-dominated semi-colonial state. In fact, beginning in the late part of the first decade, literature making these war aims explicit began to appear in the British press—even as the German military built up a war machine that made it clear that aggression against it could never return to the people its costs.

A leader in this move to destroy and colonize Germany was Winston Churchill, the future prime minister of Britain who would destroy its empire in the century's second genocidal, fratricidal war. Churchill had been a war correspondent in the British campaign against the independent Boer states in southern Africa, and had come under fire in a number of colonial engagements, particularly in Sudan and India, before that. Militarily, he had little skill, and his greatest achievement had been his escape from a Boer prison camp after his capture in the Boer War. Yet Churchill was an ardent British imperialist, as well as a drunk, and always willing to call for war without thinking of how war might impact the people of the British empire. He was a useful tool of the Jews, and the Jews made sure he won a place in Parliament.

America, still nominally independent, was less sure of the wisdom of this, but France, smarting from the defeat inflicted on it by Germany during the War of German Unification which Bismarck had directed in the 1870s, was more than willing to act against its perceived ethnic enemy. The other nations of Europe and America wanted little or no involvement in yet another aggressive war. Austria was troubled by communist-backed "nationalist" movements and Russia was simply a giant behemoth, glad to be too poor to be an attractive target for the Jews. Italy had no stake in any conflict with Germany, and America was still in the infancy of being dragged into the world system—its Eastern Establishment wanted what Britain wanted, but the South, Midwest and West were still rapidly developing—many of them only recently growing or having grown to the point they could qualify for statehood—and had their own interests, which didn't include "deleting excess workers" as casualties in a banker's war.

Germany, too, had little interest in a war, except as a means of preserving its existence. It didn't wish to be swallowed up by the British empire, or to become a semi-colonial state under foreign domination, and was well aware of the aggressive intentions of its neighbors. It also recognized the threat posed to it by the politics of Masons and Jewish radicals, those radicals having led the uprisings that had challenged Prussian dominance in each of the major upheavals of the 19th century. Germany was a monarchy, and to remain a monarchy and to preserve the traditional European way of life it had to resist and defeat efforts to impose upon it socialism and democracy. But Germany was a united nation of German people, the only other Germanic nation on the continent being Austria, and thus it had no motive and little practical desire to expand its borders to incorporate other peoples.

There was tension though between Germany and Russia on the Polish question. Poland had begun its life in post-medieval Europe united with Lithuania, a major power in the east, and the last nation to remain pagan, not converting to Christianity until the 14th century. Poland/Lithuania had fought with Germany almost since the moment of its inception, and had early on conquered and destroyed the Teutonic Knights, the ethnically German religious order that had led the Crusades against the eastern Slavic peoples. Yet, in the 19th century, Poland had been definitively destroyed by its neighbors, with the bulk of its nation given to Russia as a province, and the northern coastal area it claimed affirmed in the hands of the German states and Prussia.

Russia, like Austria, was a multi-cultural empire, and, as such, it had no limit to its greed for new lands. Unlike Germany, which was an essentially national state, in that it united peoples of one ethnicity—German—in one nation, much like France had when the theory of "petty bourgeois nationalism" was first posited, Russia had conquered foreign peoples all the way to Pacific, and, as such, was constructed in a way that would not limit its ability to attack a free and independent people and subjugate them.

This territorial dispute between Germany and Russia over the lands claimed by Poland was the root of the Slavic-Nordic conflict that appeared in racial writings of the early 20th century. As with many things, theory was made a slave to politics, and the natural division within the white race between dolicocephalic (long-headed) and brachiocephalic (round-headed) peoples was expanded into a conflict between the Germanic peoples and the Slavs, who were written out of the white race and turned into racial enemies—a terrible distortion of the truth.

This kind of ethnic distortion is similar to that which wrote the Irish out of the white race in Britain and the United States during the middle and late 19th centuries, and the Italians out in the late 19th and early 20th centuries. Here, it was a petty national conflict between the British empire and Ireland that lay at this racial distortion's root.

These kinds of ethnic splits within the white race were once a major crack in the racial edifice which the Jews used to divide and conquer white people and seize control of Europe, America and the white world. The Irish Republican Army, for instance, was a proto-communist organization that had Jewish leadership in much of the late 19th and early 20th century, and is today a major force in Ireland fighting for the conversion of that nation from a white into a colored nation. Having defeated the hated white British and won Irish independence, the Jews of the Irish Republican Army now seek to invite in Negroes and have the country conquered by non-white immigration. Even today in the United States, those among the large Irish minority who incline toward nationalist or racialist views are often coaxed by the Jews into a faux-"Celtic" pride that is defined by opposition to the other white races and the "embracing of diversity," with no conception that such faux-nationalism is no different than the Negro communism of China or black Africa.

Similarly, Russian, Polish, and German ethnic hatred and divisions were manipulated by the Jews during the First and Second World War to allow them to seize control of eastern Europe. What was essentially a territorial dispute between petty-national entities was turned into an international flash point that prohibited two nations with shared ethnic and political interests from uniting to fight the common enemy, which was the international Jewish-led move toward revolution, communism and democracy.

Thus when World War I came, one monarchist nation in Europe—Russia—was brought over to the side of Britain and France, and destroyed by their choice, just as they destroyed their fellow monarchies and ended Europe's period of normality, and beginning the end of time.

The spark of World War I was a relatively petty thing—the Archduke Ferdinand, a member of Austria's ruling Hapsburg family, was assassinated by a Jewish anarchist acting under the cloak of Slavic and Serbian nationalism.

As with the tensions between Germany and Russia over the territory claimed by Poland, the conflict between the Austrian Hapsburgs and the territories claimed by the ethnicities of their empire had been painted in terms of German versus Slav. This division had been encouraged by Russia, who had positioned itself as the ethnic champion of Slavs, though its ruling family, the Romanovs, were also Germanic in origin, and who saw championing the ethnic causes of Slavs as a means of expanding its territory into the Balkans. In furtherance of this policy, the Russians had allied with Serbia and utilized their secret police to support leftist and Jewish movements in Austria that had co-opted Slavic nationalism. Thus Croatians, Slovenians, Bosnians, Bohemians, Czechs and Slovaks were urged by the Russians to revolt against Austrian rule as a prelude to expanding the boundaries of the Russian empire.

Austria began shelling Serbia's capital of Belgrade about a month and a half after the assassination, and its act of war was immediately capitalized upon by Russia, which issued statements attacking the entirety of the German race. Just as the Jews manipulated ethnic rivalries between whites to unseat white governments and disempower white people in internal politics, the blinded monarchs of decadent Europe used such policies to launch a genocidal war, whose spark has been set off by Jewish agitators. Once Russia began issuing ethnic threats against the German people, Germany could no longer stand by and allow the conflict between Austria and Serbia to remain a local affair. Germany had to stand in solidarity with Austria because Russia's faux-Slavic imperialism involved a threat of war and genocide against the German people—and on this basis, with Russian troops mobilizing at the German border, Germany ordered Russia to demobilize and then declared war when Russia refused.

Thus World War I began not as a war of democracy against monarchy, but a closely orchestrated conflict between monarchs, instigated on racial grounds, by Jewish-communist revolutionaries who sought to destroy all three powers (Germany, Austria and Russia) and bring them under the Jewish-communist-democratic yoke.

France and Russia were in alliance against Germany, and Britain had been contemplating a war to subjugate Germany to the British economic system for several decades. France declared war on Germany in support of Russia, and British, in preparation for an invasion of Germany, approached Belgium and asked permission to deploy British troops in Belgian territory to attack the German state. Upon learning of this intent, Germany declared war on Belgium and occupied it, and the pretext for war—German "aggression" against "innocent" Belgium, was given to "the democracies"—the united international Freemasonic systems of Britain and France.

In the United States, world Jewry pretended not to know which side they wished to take, as none of the combatants on the eastern front were quite to their taste. All of them had been accused of anti-Semitism, and the Jews had begun the early stages of their "holocaust" propaganda in the late 19th century with claims that the reason for Jewish emigration into Germany and the United States was "pogroms" that were being conducted against them by Russians and by Poles. Of course, no such pogroms existed—there were local revolts against Jewish usurers and a concerted effort by the Russian government to suppress Jewish-led communist movements, but no general persecution of the Jewish people led to their migration into Germany—just the opportunity to exploit a nation economically that had been created by the opening of the Jewish ghettoes by the German state.

The United States has always been a more German nation than English, and by the early 20th century, as now, its largest ethnic groups were Germans and Irish (in fact, there are more Germans and more Irish and more "mixed German-Irish" citizens in the United States than even Mexicans, the third-largest ethnic group in the country as of 2010). Further, there was a strong sense, even among Americans of British descent, that America should remain out of European conflicts, as it remained out of the international money system until 1913. But the second decade of the century had brought enough changes in the American mentality that this voice, while still loud, was not able to drown out the forces of war.

As the war in Europe progressed, it was clear that Germany was stronger than Britain, France and Russia combined—as would be the case in the second genocidal war of that century. The war ground down to a stalemate, and millions were ground up in suicidal charges against machine guns as trench fighting defined the warfare of the Western Front. The cry went out for America to join the war, as more force was needed to destroy Germany, and as it became clear that the system of democracy was itself becoming threatened by monarchy, the Masons in the United States began to listen.

Throughout the war, the British war effort had been financed by American banks. While strong, the Bank of London and its Jews were not able to provide the British government with the amount of capital and material needed to fight the German state. To rectify this, the British turned to the Morgans, their old allies, as well as a coalition of American banking families, to provide "loans" to them—loans that were guaranteed by the U.S. government and eventually forgiven. This war would, in fact, be the shining moment of the Anglo-banking families in the United States, as it became evident early on that the decision of the United States to maintain a decentralized banking system had made the U.S. government unable to finance the Jews' foreign wars on their own. This is a defect that was be rectified before the second genocidal war of the century, and was a major factor in pushing the increased integration of the United States with the British-based international banking system through Congress.

The major German error of the war was sending the communist disease into Russia in the person of Vladimir Lenin, a quarter-Jewish communist revolutionary who had fled to Europe to escape arrest after the aborted coup efforts of the first decade of the century. Though Germany understood its ethnic allegiance to Austria and the ideological danger it faced on the Western Front, its monarchs were unable to see the depth of the Jew's schemes in manipulating a war between Germans and Slavs, democracies and monarchies, and lacked the ideological framework to understand the place communism held among its enemies. The German Kaiser could not see the Jew as international, and thus he misunderstood the communist struggle in Russia as a purely national affair. Thus, when the Russian government, defeated, was forced to surrender, the Kaiser released Lenin like a plague bacteria into the Russian empire.

Lenin was, of course, welcomed by his fellow Jews, and by the international system of Jewry, both capitalist and communist in name. Once he entered Russia, he was greeted by a host of international bankers, Kuhn, Loeb and Company, most prominent among them who rushed to hand him "loans" to finance his violent and genocidal struggle against the Russian people. After the defeat of Russia, the czar had instituted a parliament, much in the manner of the doomed Louis XVI of France, but, as in France, within this parliament the radical factions led by the Jews quickly overcame both the ethnically Russian monarchists and then the more moderate Jews, and pushed a program of genocide and regicide through into law. Not content with the half-measure of democracy, Lenin and his Jewish compatriots, including the gang of criminals around Stalin and the triad of Trotsky, Kamenev and Zinoviev, seized the government and touched off a civil war whose chaos would give them the pretext to create the total Jewish state—the Union of Soviet Socialist Republics.

The empowerment of Jewish communists in Russia also gave strength to Jewish communists in Germany, and the communist movement, which was encouraged by the nominally "capitalist" West for the same reasons that communism in Russia had been given a push in its infancy by monarchist Germany, was able to derail and eventually defeat the war effort.

For four years the best of Europe's men were ground away into nothing in the fields of slaughter created for them by the Jews. As millions were returned to dirt and as blood ran in rivers across the plains of Western Europe, the Jews saw the decimation of the white race as an opportunity to make their move, shunt aside their Masonic allies and emerge as the world controllers they had spent two millennia aspiring to be. War, when fought in defense of one's hearth and home, draws forth the best and bravest element of the race, that element of the race that is willing to sacrifice itself for the preservation of the racial whole. When this element of the race was massacred, the entire race was made vulnerable, as those who survived were more likely to be the weaker kind of element that was willing to compromise at all turns and sacrifice their fellow to preserve their mere existence for as long a duration as possible. It takes, generally, three generations to pass after such a genocidal war for the defensive anti-bodies of the racial collective to renew themselves. Thus, World War I was the prelude for a Second World War that would leave the white race powerless and without honor in its leaders into the 21st century.

Yet the peoples of America, who could easily have stood aside and allowed the war in Europe to conclude without any vital interest having been touched, were lured into battle against the irrational threat of a German invasion. Time and time again the ignorance of Americans—an ignorance born of relative geographical isolation and an extremely poor educational system—has been tapped to lead this country into war, and this was as true in the early 20th century as it is in the early 21st century, when morons boldly proclaim at the local Wal-Mart that American troops fight in Afghanistan to prevent an Afghan invasion of Appalachia. In the run-up to World War I, the American people were told that, despite the domination of the seas by the British navy and the occupation of the German people in a two front war in Europe, that there was a risk that Germany would launch troop transports against the Eastern coast of the United States. This, and British propaganda among the Eastern elite, combined with a battle call to fight for the global banking system and America's "economic interests," pushed the United States into participation and caused the death of hundreds of thousands of American youths.

Another factor in the decision for America to fight against Germany was the swing of American Jewry toward Britain that followed the Balfour declaration, which was a British diplomatic communication to world Jewry promising the Jews a nation in Palestine should the Germans be defeated.

Germany had been active in the Near East since the beginning of the 20th century, and the German Kaiser had taken a pro-Islamic policy, standing in solidarity with the Ottoman Turks, who had positioned themselves, as conquerors of the central/western part of the Muslim world, as representatives of Islam in the West. From a cynical viewpoint, the Germans and Austrians, despite the fact the Turks had once threatened Vienna and the heart of Europe, had seen the Turks and Muslims as a counterweight against the Slavs of both the Balkans and the Russian empire, and had made the alliance in support of their perceived *Realpolitik*. However, Germany had been involved in a number of development projects in the Near and Middle East, and had made alliances with Arab leaders that would not have allowed them to grant the Jews a state in Palestine, or to pressure the Turks to do so.

In contrast, the British would gain from the dismemberment of the Ottoman empire, and their gains would be substantial enough that cutting off a sliver of their colonial territory for the Jews seemed a minor thing to a government whose religion was derived from devil-worship and had no particular attachment to the Jewish holy land. It is also questionable whether the British ever had any intention of honoring their agreement with the Jews, as they did not do so until thirty years after World War I's conclusion.

A more powerful concern for world Jewry was the success of the Jewish power-grab in Russia, which would allow them not only to commit genocide against a people they had arbitrarily declared their "enemy," but would give world Jewry a much larger and more powerful base from which to launch their wars for world control. While the British promises of the Zionist homeland certainly won over many, the flood of Jews leaving the United States for Russia to participate in both the government and the struggle against the "imperialist" nations that were trying to protect the white peoples of Russia from genocide was decisive. The Jews of America threw their weight in with America's bankers and Anglo-elite, and war with Germany was declared.

With communist Jews stabbing them in the back and the minions of capitalist Jewry and the British banking system machine gunning them in the front, Germany could not stand, and its Kaiser, already too soft on socialists in that he allowed their kind to breed and grow under his rule, was forced to abdicate. With the collapse of the German monarchy came the collapse of the German war effort, and the Jews, having defeated the other monarchies of Europe, were allowed to place Germany under their boot, and descended upon it, saliva dripping from their jaws, like ravenous cannibals or blood-crazed zombies seeking to eviscerate and devour their victim.

The result of the defeat of Germany and of monarchy was a series of "red" revolutions across Europe that devoured the ethnicities they sought to liberate, as well as a formal system of British and French economic control over Germany that re-

Kaiser Wilhelm II was one of the last members of the European aristocracy to hold power in Europe. A Hohenzollern, with the Hapsburgs of Austria, he represented one of the oldest lineages on the continent—so he and his Austrian counterparts had to be expelled from power by the democracies.

duced the German empire to a British colonial state, similar in many ways to the position that had been held by Ireland. In Hungary, the same Hungarian "nationalism" that had led to the revolution against Austrian rule in 1848 turned into Jewish government under Bela Kun, and the Hungarian people were faced with genocide until they united and overthrew the Jewish monster. In Bavaria, the Spartacists, a Jewish-led communist faction that had also grown out of the revolutionary movements of 1848, briefly seized power, and it was in the blood of this monster that many of the storm troopers of the coming nationalist movement were baptized. And in France, the Versailles Treaty was signed, and the British and French began their program of plunder and rapine against the German people.

The chimera was a mythical beast with the heads of a goat, a serpent and a lion incorporated into its body. The lion symbolizes the brutal god Baal, scion of democracy. The serpent is the Egyptian Apep, scion of communism. The goat is the god of the Jews, Seth-Yahweh, and is the Zionist beast. Above, a clay relief depicts a Greek culture hero battling a chimera.

CHAPTER FOUR

THE JEWISH CENTURY

After the defeat of Germany and Austria and the overthrow of the Russian government during World War I, the old normative institutions of Europe had been completely annihilated by the democratic and communist forces of revolution, and the mission that the Jews had begun in the 17th century, with their overthrow of the British monarchy and their institutionalization of Masonic power, had been completed. The social structures necessary for white resistance to Jewish occupation had been annihilated, and the destructive and poisonous cultural tendency of these anti-people had free rein.

It is no surprise, then, that the interwar period is the period in which the modern financial system of capitalism and the first experiments in centralized economic control were placed into practice in Europe. Prior to World War I, the British had attempted a world economic system through their system of exploitation of their colonies and centralized control of money and exchange in their Bank of London. Yet many nations had remained independent of this system, and total economic control had proved elusive. One issue had been the fact that the economic system had become associated with the British nation—and it was this issue that the clique around the *London Times* and the Rhodes groups of Round Tables had sought to address with their nominal decolonization. Yet even this approach to centralized world control was inadequate for the Jews because it left the goyim with significant power. And though the power of whites had been greatly reduced by the slaughter of white people that had occurred during World War I, it had not yet been completely broken. Thus, the major goal of the Jews in the interwar period was to discard and push aside their white allies in the capitalist world and to establish themselves as the true puppet masters of the world economy.

The sanctions program that was instituted against Germany by Britain and France is what would become the model for the economic rapine that characterized the second half of the 20th century. France and Britain entered Germany at the invitation of the Jewish-controlled German socialist parties and literally packed the factories and equipment of the German industrial base into boxes and shipped them back to their home countries. France physically occupied the Rhineland and seized its industrial production. The German government was ordered to make payments to the capitalist nations that exceeded the remaining productive power of the German economy, and the German nation was placed into a state of perpetual bankruptcy.

The administrator of this program was the Jew-capitalist ideologue Ludwig von Mises, who would later become an icon of the American libertarian movement, after spawning a group of Jewish economists who would go on to dominate the American Federal Reserve. Von Mises was a Jew in the service of the Bank of London who, after his time administrating the German reparations program, would go on to head the Austrian central bank—from which position he was expelled by a mob of the Austrian workers he exploited in what the Jews today claim was an act of "Nazi terror."

The effort to bring Germany into the world economy as a colony of the British banking system was paralleled with the first effort to create a one world government under the domination of the "democracies," and, as with the economy, Britain in particular. This first effort at what is now the United Nations was the League of Nations, and what caused it to fail was the refusal of the United States to participate—a refusal that showed that America had still not been sufficiently devastated by the ravages of the Jews' wars to give total submission to an order dominated by a nation much of America viewed with suspicion. These failures would contribute to the Jewish decision to dump Britain as a base of operations and to replace it on the international scene with the United States.

Meanwhile, as the Jews on the capitalist side of the divide attempted to internationalize the British system, the Jews on the communist side were spreading revolution and instituting Jewish power throughout eastern Europe and Asia, as well as among the Negroes of the United States. After a brief and half-hearted struggle with the capitalist West, which, devastated by war and caring little about eastern Europe, had little heart to commit itself against the communist plague which was consuming Russia, the Jews established themselves throughout eastern Europe, defeating tough opposition from ethnic-nationalist socialists like Nestor Makhno in Ukraine, and losing control of the former Russian territory of Poland. Their first act upon seizing power was to appropriate all of the wealth of the Russian nation, a process that involved several stages over the next two decades, sparking a massive famine that murdered six million before the formal genocide against the non-Jewish peoples of Russia could begin. As discussed in the previous chapter, the success of Jewish power in the new Soviet Union led to Jewish-communist uprising throughout Europe, most notably the regime of Bela Kun in Hungary and the brief commune in Munich, before the capitalist powers were able to reassert themselves.

In the United States, the National Association for the Advancement of Colored People had become a totally rabbinical operation, its board consisting solely and entirely of Jews, and its early agitation against the people of the Southern United States, still culturally independent of the Yankee north, led to a revival of the Ku Klux Klan. Black racial agitation still lacked a popular base, and it was clear that another war was going to be required to change the mentality of the United States and set it on a course of self-destruction.

In Asia, after conquering the Islamic peoples of central Asia and brutally suppressing the religion of Islam, the Jews began to set their sights on China and the nations of the Far East, establishing a Chinese Communist Party which would go on to overthrow the nationalist regime imposed by the Western powers. Anti-colonial agitation was a war that the Jews chose to fight against a West already looking to grant nominal "autonomy" to the dark peoples of the world, and the racial rhetoric developed in the instigation of division in the United States served the Jews well on the international plane, where "third world revolution" would become the mantra of a later generation of red agitators.

The action of this period, though, was in Germany and central Europe, where the peoples trapped under the dual threat of capitalist democracy and communist genocide sought a third way—a way out of the pincer trap that had been set for them by the Jews. A young corporal who had served in the German military during World War I and who was now contemplating the danger that the two sides of the Hebrew posed to Germany was emerging, and the situation in Germany heightened his sense of the injustice he must battle and the mission he had been sent into the world to accomplish. This young leader was Adolf Hitler, and he would go on to become the only light shining in a century of red darkness, so hated by the Jews for his inner goodness that, generations after the end of their war against him, they would still raise youth to revile his name.

As we have discussed, in the Ancient Tradition of the Aryan peoples, there is a knowledge that time is the great destroyer. Nothing can stand before time—its ravages reduce all things to nothing, end all life, and destroy all of creation. Time is cyclic—its decline occurs in definite stages that can be measured and predicted—and after its end it returns to the state of its beginning—but while it is degenerating forward it cannot be stopped. And when one realizes the unconquerable nature of the god the Vedic Hindus called Mahakala, the question becomes how one chooses to understand and relate to this.

Savitri Devi, the great thinker of the war period, has said there are three relationships man can have toward time—he can choose to live in it, he can choose to live above it, or he can choose to live against it. Those who live in time are those who deceive themselves with the myth of progress—who see the marching forward of time not as a great death, but a great act forward—a necessary step for the "advancement of man," in the way a man walking the plank advances toward the chaos of the sea. This position, which is the position all of lesser humanity takes, is a position in its essence of denial—denial of the inevitable destruction of one's nature, and the embrace of death. The Jews are the philosophers of this death par excellence; they lead the charge forward into the inevitable nothingness of the future.

Those who live above time become timeless by removing themselves from the care of this world. They focus on the timeless within themselves and seek a perfection of the eternal nature—of the spirit—and a disregard or discarding of the bodily frame. Jesus the Christ and the Buddha are two examples of the man above time—the man who has found such perfection within himself that he is insensible to time's ravages, and who can live eternally because he has transcended his bodily existence and become part of the spiritual substance of which man partakes.

But the greatest of men are those who live against time—who, realizing the futility and hopelessness of their struggle, and the inevitably of their own death, fight against time and its minions in this world in an effort to stop the inevitable death of man. This caste—the Aryan warrior caste—is the class of man that rises to Valhalla, and who lives forever awaiting the final battle, where they will burn with the destruction of the world but, in doing so, allow the world to rise against from the ashes. They realize that the sacrifice of the self in this world is necessary for the regeneration and rejuvenation of an existence hopelessly corrupted by the spirit of modernism—of time's infection of the human soul.

These men are led by the great Aryan father—the sky god, Dyaus; the eternal Sun, Re; the storm god Odin who leads men into the final battle knowing that he will die so that the world again can live. In the Vedas this is Vishnu, and Vishnu comes to the world periodically in his avatars, who, in a period of chaos, when it seems that the world cannot be redeemed and all struggle is hopeless, are invested with the power to reverse the flow forward of time and, for a brief moment, restore to the world the beauty of the order that was given man in the first time and which will belong to mankind again.

In the 20th century, Adolf Hitler was the avatar of Vishnu, a living manifestation of god on Earth, and those who battled against him were the army of demons, led by the troll-women, the serpents and the evil gods of the storm, who sought to destroy mankind. Adolf Hitler was not the savior—he was not the last one. And Devi tells us Hitler was aware that he was not to be the last one, for as he stood at the balcony of the clock tower in Vienna, having been inspired by Wagner's opera, he told his close friend and companion that he knew he had been given a mission by God, and that he was the means by which God was to come into the world, but he was not to be that last one, but the one who was to make way for the last one, who would fight the final battle, destroy all of the demons, fall in battle, and restore the Golden Age which man had lost.

Thus Hitler, like Christ, was both a man and a divinity upon the Earth—that rare being who was able to make himself the vessel by which the eternal forces of order were able to enter a world consumed by chaos and reassert themselves. As a man, like Christ, he was fallible, and the temptations of the devil and his time in the wilderness were what burned away the chaff and base metal of his soul, allowing himself to become pure gold, all the way into the last moment when he sacrificed himself for the redemption of man and played his necessary role in falling to the heads of the Jewish beast.

Economically, Germany—and the rest of central Europe—in the interwar period was much like America today. Its industrial base was hollowed out—not voluntarily, through trade agreements, but involuntarily, through reparations and armed forces—and its people, unable to work in their own land because of the presence of foreigners, were compelled to mortgage their assets and borrow to attempt to maintain their standard of living. After the brief period of chaos that immediately followed the war, this led to the system of the rentenmark which, like the late American dollar, was primarily backed by the ability of the German people to borrow against their real estate. When the Great Depression hit, as in the United States, there was a massive wave of foreclosure as foreign and Jewish speculators seized the security for their debts. Unlike America, where a black-communist regime today ruthlessly exploits the white workers, in Germany, there was a nationalist alternative, and this alternative is what restored stability to the country.

The causes of the Great Depression were multi-fold, but

what it essentially represented was the failure of the British system of international exchange, which, as with the American system in modern times, encouraged an overexpansion of credit that was allowed to artificially inflate the value of assets—particularly stocks—and thus caused a crash when the ability to borrow exceeded the ability to produce income. It was complemented in the United States by climatic events that caused massive crop failures in what was essentially an agrarian economy, and exacerbated by the recent centralization of the banking system and its integration with its cousins of London and Paris.

Essentially, to create the false appearance of wealth, the Jews, through their banks, extended credit to individuals to buy and invest in companies to a greater degree than those companies could produce a return. This simple economic act is the root cause of most economic cycles—predicting the extent of credit (debt) an economy can handle is a difficult act, and the inability of man to do so causes economic fluctuations as the success or failure of his endeavors grows or contracts the economy. But the deliberate overextension of credit with the intent of causing a general economic failure goes back to Joseph and his theft of the goods of the people of Egypt—they wait for the iron to grow hot, for all the calamities of nature and economic miscalculation to compound each other, and then they strike.

So when the world economy collapsed, the Jews struck like serpents and seized, in the United States and around the world, control of the organs of the mass media, while pushing into office candidates that assisted them in centralizing economic control and formalizing the exploitation of the people. The Jews bought up the newspapers and the new, powerful, companies that were broadcasting on radio, just as they had once gained control of the theaters and the entertainment industry. Their theater business had already bought them into Hollywood, and they had made allies across the nation with the criminal organizations that had recently immigrated to America from the Italian peninsula, giving them muscle with which to enforce their tightening grip on the people of the United States. The growing movie industry was controlled by Jewish studios, along with the theater chains that displayed them, and now the old newspapers of the country, once partisan instruments in the hands of the regional gentile powers of North and South, were forced into bankruptcy by the banker's Depression and then forced into the hands of their new Hebrew owners.

The power of the press could not be overestimated, and the Zionist segment of the Jews had already learned this lesson with their postwar campaign for "the first holocaust"—the alleged starvation of six million Jews in Poland after World War I. Though little remembered now, during the Russian Revolution, Polish nationalism had become a major enemy of the communist revolution, and, during the chaos of the dissolution of Russia, Poland had been able to both break free and remain free from the red communist terror that seized its neighbor. This had infuriated the Jews, and as they had struggled that armed struggle which they had believed may bring them to world power through world workers revolution, their organs in the United States, particularly the *New York Times*, would loudly denounce the "holocaust" which the Jews of Poland were experiencing as the anti-communist fighters of that land exterminated their communist enemies. "Six million" were said to have died in the fighting—a number as false as the "other" six million which would follow it—but tens of millions were raised for Zionist and Jewish aid foundations that were allegedly assisting the survivors of this mass famine in fleeing to better pastures, including the British protectorate of Palestine.

So, as paper after paper across the United States fell into Jewish hands—the beginnings of the so-called "left-wing" media—and the growing radio and movie industry became or remained

Jewish productions, the political system in the United States underwent a profound change, as a Jew and communist sympathizer, Franklin D. Roosevelt, assumed the presidency for life—the first and last American leader (so far) to have done so.

Roosevelt built himself up on the backs of the poor, and on the exploitation of the hopes and fears of a people caught in an economic trap that many of them could not comprehend. Much of his economic program was good—in fact, much of his economic program was an imitation of the National Socialist German economic program he would decry—but its core was evil. Not a nationalist but an internationalist, Roosevelt's power grab represented the opposite of what the National Socialist ascension represented just as evil represent the opposite of good, though the two, at times, may use similar methods.

The distinction between national and international socialist is often not well understood, and, in the United States, where anti-socialist rhetoric is a norm of the nominal "right," an effort has been made to deliberately obscure the two. Socialism is merely the direction of the economy by the state in the interest of the workers, and it is absolutely necessary, as the state is nothing but force, and, in modern times, force can often be bought with money—thus, if the state cannot regulate the money and the means by which it is gathered and accumulated, then the state can be destroyed. The question is not whether the state regulates commerce—all states have always done so— the question is how the state chooses to regulate commerce and economic activity.

The internationalist approach regulates the economy in the benefit of everyone –of the "international community," a notion so broad as to have no meaning—and thus regulates it only in the interests of the class which controls the state. As Max Stirner noted, the state in such a society exists only to perpetuate itself, and it becomes, as man can become, a creature

President Franklin Delano Roosevelt was intent on starting a war to spread democracy and socialism into the heart of Central Europe. Allied with the forces of British capitalism, he arranged for Germany's Japanese allies to attack the United States, in order to drag the United States into war against German Europe. Above, FDR gives his first inaugural address.

"in time"—an apparatus existing only to perpetuate the class or clique which controls it for as long as possible before it self-destructs and dies.

In contrast, the national direction of the economy is precisely that—the direction of the economy in the interest of the "national" whole. While this "national" whole can be defined in the petty bourgeois sense as being all people within the arbitrary borders of the nation, as we have discussed previously, such a definition is useless, because each people represents a different ethno-cultural organism, and thus has inherently different interests. These interests may include some form of cooperation with each other, but they cannot involve the same set of norms and mores that are a prerequisite for any meaningful notion of law.

Thus when the "national" is united with the "racial," the nation is defined naturally as a people, and the economy is directed in that people's social interest, rather than exploiting the mass of the people for the benefit of a small clique, the state becomes an instrument through which the people can live and be given life. It becomes the natural expression of the collective will. Instead of an engine of destruction it becomes an engine of creation, and the masses of the people, unthinking herd that they are, have their inertia turned into momentum as their collective charge forward is used to sustain, rather than destroy, the life impetus of the cultural organism.

To put it simply, the international state is a lie designed to serve the ethnic interest of the Jew, whereas the national state serves the interest of the people it governs. The difference between the two is that of the difference of a gun in the hands of a murderer and of the man who kills the murderer. In opposition to the common American belief, the state is merely a tool—just as the gun is a tool—and the manner in which the tool is used is more important than the nature of the tool itself. A good tool used badly will never produce a good result, whereas a bad tool wielded with good intention can often be forced into its new role.

Thus the ascension of Adolf Hitler in Germany infused the German people—regardless of their national boundaries—with life, and, with their newfound life, they found prosperity and power which, only years before, had seemed impossible to even hope for. Hitler is associated in the West with war, but the massive extent of his social programs and his working class economic reforms are what truly separated him from both the capitalist and communist systems. Few know it, but the first act of Hitler's National Socialist Workers' Party was the Winter Relief drive, which was a massive charitable effort to stop Germans from starving and freezing to death in the terrible northern winter. It was a moral effort, but it drew the people together and taught them that their role in society was to help each other, not fight each other, thus setting the tone for the next twelve years of National Socialist power.

After the communists burned the German parliament—and there is no need to believe the Soviet lie that the "Nazis" burned it themselves, though that lie has been repeated so often it has often gained credence—Hitler was able to consolidate power in the face of the armed forces that, trained and equipped by Soviet intelligence, were plotting the overthrow of the state. In the face of this danger, Hitler imprisoned approximately 25,000 of the most violent and anti-social of the communists—a majority of them Jewish—and sentenced them to six to 12 months in minimum security German prison camps. The Jews internationally denounced this as a "holocaust," akin to mass executions and genocide.

Hitler's main reforms were for the German worker. His most important was to stabilize the economy on a mixed bag of industrial production, rather than on debt and the mortgaging of land. Hitler canceled the foreclosures and property seizures which Jewish and British bankers and land speculators had indulged in under the Weimar Republic, and returned small farms and small businesses to the farmers and businessmen who operated them—another act decried by the dispossessed Jews as "genocide." He brought together the great companies of Germany and persuaded them to issue bonds in conjunction with the Reichsbank that backed the new Reichsmark, and thus, where, in the United States, Franklin Roosevelt was imposing a tax on American labor to pay the Jewish bankers of the Federal Reserve, Hitler was paying for his goods out of the productive activities of the German industrial base.

Hitler also put the German people back to work through a

massive program of infrastructure development which brought about the autobahn and the communications and transport system the German economy needed to grow. In America, there are fools who argue that roads should be privatized, and that all investment by the government in its own country is futile, but there is no question that government investment in projects that cannot be conducted by industry because their produce is the common property of the people can improve and grow a nation's economic base. Thus Roosevelt attempted to imitate Hitler in this, establishing a variety of work programs under the authority of the National Recovery Act.

While putting money into the hands of German workers through millions of new jobs, Hitler also put property in the hands of the people by offering low-interest government-subsidized loans to working people that were canceled upon the birth of children. Every time a German working family had a child, one-fourth of their mortgage debt was forgiven, on the rationale—which proved correct—that a German child consumed and produced enough goods that his or her economic activity more than compensated society for the debt. Imagine in the United States if having four white children allowed you to own a house—instead of creating an economic burden that could cause a house to go into foreclosure. It goes almost without saying that Hitler ended the German birth problem—the falling birth rates associated with economic failure—within half a decade.

Hitler did impose racial and eugenic laws, and, like his economic reforms, these were for the good of the German nation. He forbade Jews from engaging in certain intellectual and cultural activities that are essential to molding the consciousness of the nation. Jews could not—except in a very limited fashion—work in the newspaper industry or the mass media; they could not teach Germans at public universities, and they could not engage in seditious political, economic or social activity—communist agitation, usurious banking, and trafficking in sex, abortion and prostitutes being the most prominent example of each. They were otherwise free—and, if they did not like the German nation, they were free to leave to it and to go to one of the nations they had created—the United States or the Soviet Union—to enjoy the benefits of the societies they had made. Many Jews chose to do so—and with them, they brought forth tales of the "holocaust" they had barely escaped—the "genocide" of being unable to poison and to murder the souls of the innocent, and the "oppression" of being denied the instruments by which they could torture society.

Hitler also strove to improve the German people through his eugenics program. Contrary to popular belief, very few Germans were euthanized—humanely executed—because of genetic defect. Anyone who could work or who was reasonably supported or able to support themselves was allowed to live, often to the horror of those who advocated the mass euthanization of the underclass. Only those so seriously disabled that they could neither enjoy life nor participate in it were humanely dispatched. Many others who had genetic defects, particularly alcoholism, were sterilized but permitted to live.

The belief that mere biological existence is the highest value in life, as opposed to full participation in the transcendent and the elevation of life above the material, is a belief that is essentially Christian, and is a product of the world-destroying soul of the Christian religion—a soul that Christianity inherits from Judaism. The Christian believes that all mankind is so far below God that the differences between men are eclipsed, and that the highest elements of the race and the lowest elements of the race should be reduced to the same misery. This is also the guiding belief of communism, and the foundation of the bridge communism has built to Christianity.

Life, though, demands something more of man than a mere existence, devoid of pleasure, spent begging for a forgiveness that never comes until the organism itself has been destroyed. The essentially heathen belief of the Aryan is that man can rise above his station and beyond the confines of the material body to the divine world in this lifetime—that he can become a vessel by which god and the divine are channeled into the world, and, that, through this channeling, the initial creative act which imbued the world with life is recreated, and life is reaffirmed and given birth anew. But there are those biological organisms which have lost that ability because they are so damaged, whether by genetic defect or accident, that they cannot ever transcend themselves, nor can they be useful in the maintenance of the life of those others who are capable of transcendence. When life becomes mere biological existence, when all opportunity to be better than one is, is denied, and when one cannot even play a role in the social mechanism that allows others to strive to the higher state of being, then the kindest thing society can do is end that biological existence, remembering the words of Marcus Aurelius that death is no harm because it is inevitable, and that it is the suffering of an existence lived in pain, and not death, which is the true source of evil.

That Hitler was an opponent of alcoholism, and that alcoholism was one of the offenses for which a man or woman could be sterilized, would probably shock many of the beer-swilling street nationalists of today. But understanding this objection is to understand the nature of the distortion by which the National Socialist philosophy has been turned into another manifestation of the death force in the modern world. Few today who claim to be "neo-Nazis" celebrate the beauty of the National Socialist state. Instead, many "neo-Nazis" accept the modernist lie that National Socialism was responsible for World War II and for the genocide of the Jewish people, and advocate it. Believing National Socialism to be associated with cruelty, pain, the infliction of suffering and death, they pair with it the habits of those who live their lives dedicated to the destruction of the world, including the use of those mind-numbing substances which suppress mankind's natural humanity and allow the expression of his most base nature. In the latter part of the 20th century, this became known as "drugs, death and the devil," and into this anti-human philosophy the Jewish account of National Socialist Germany was woven.

Through his economic reforms, and through his intolerance for evil, lies and those people who devoted themselves to the spreading of evil and lies, Hitler was able to remove Germany from the British-capitalist system, while preventing anger at that system to be manipulated by the Jews into its partner, Bolshevism. In measured steps, Hitler restored Germany to its proper place in the world, and began to reunite all of the German peoples of Europe into a single and properly national state.

The postwar borders of Europe were set by the League of Nations based upon the petty-bourgeois "national" principle, and these borders reflected more the greed of various local segments of the international capitalist elite than the actual ethnic divisions of the European people. Freemasonry had dictated that, all people being the same and equal, the nation was merely an arbitrary collection of people, and thus national borders need not reflect ethnic or racial divisions. Thus the German population of Europe was divided among several lands—primarily Germany and Austria, but also Switzerland, Czechoslovakia, Poland and the historically German communities of now Soviet Russia. The Germans of Soviet Russia were lost—as a productive economic caste, the Jews had taken to their extermination, and Germany was not powerful enough yet to attempt their rescue. But the recently divorced German peoples of Austria, the Czech Republic and Poland were within reach of

National Socialist Germany, and properly belonged in the German state. Thus, Hitler strove to unite them.

The question of the 19th century had been whether the German states would be united under Prussian or Austrian leadership, and whether Prussia and Austria would be able to reconcile their differences enough to unite along ethnic lines. That Austria was not a German nation had never been brought into question until the Jews produced *The Sound of Music* and the British grew afraid that Germany united with its southeastern province would be too strong. Yet the British, blinded by the Jews within their midst to the Jewish problem and the threat of communist Jewish totalitarianism, remained captive to the policies of world economic domination that they had pursued during the Victorian period—the same policies that had started the disastrous war that had spelled the beginning of the end of their political and economic power.

In Austria there was a "fascist" leader—a dictator named Engelbert Dollfuss who was imposing capitalist economic policies and Jewish central banking on the Austrian people without and against their consent—and Ludwig von Mises, now removed from the reparations program, was the representative of Zion in his cabinet. But Adolf Hitler sought something more for the Austrian peasants and workers than to turn over the hard-earned product of their labor to some ephemeral Hebrew conglomerate, and this promise is what motivated the uprisings and riots that brought down the Austrian state and led to a victory for unification with Germany in the Austrian plebiscite.

Germany's absorption of Austria was not an aggressive act, and no European power saw it as such—just as Germany's reoccupation of the Rhineland was seen as a necessary and inevitable end to what had been a terrible and wrongfully conceived insult to the German nation. By uniting his people under one government, Adolf Hitler did not want war with other white peoples—he merely wanted to fulfill the role that God had granted him. In fact, peace and unified pursuit of the interests of the white race were Adolf Hitler's priorities with Britain, whose people he realized were of the same stock as himself and his beloved Germans.

But Britain, blinded by the lies of its enemies within, could not see German unification as anything but a threat to its irrational, unjust and unsustainable goal of total world control, and one of the many steps it took in response to the German reunification with Austria was to threaten to place bomber bases in Czechoslovakia from which it would inflict genocide on the German people. Hitler already sought to restore the Germans of the Sudentenland to the Fatherland—their alienation was a result of the Versailles Treaty—and it was the will of Czechoslovakia's German minority that they be united with their brothers once again. The British threats brought this issue to a head, and Hitler knew that, to prevent his encirclement by the murderous forces of his misguided northern European brethren, he had to act. Thus preparations for an occupation of the German regions of Czechoslovakia were made.

Originally, Hitler sought a multi-lateral peace agreement—one in which Poland, Hungary and Germany would work jointly to resolve the problems of the Czechs and the Slovaks and the German, Polish and Hungarian minorities that had been forced into the Czechoslovak state. His policies were also popular with the Slovaks, who felt unjustly dominated by their Czech neighbors, who controlled a more prosperous portion of the country and who were more firmly in the British camp. On the verge of such a peace conference, British intervention prevented the Hungarian and Polish states from participation, and Hitler knew that Germany would have to act unilaterally to preserve peace in the region.

It is hard, with the manner in which the occupation of

Czechoslovakia is understood today, to realize the depth of the danger the German people in Czech borders faced. With both sides still brainwashed with the divisive anti-Slav/anti-German propaganda of World War I, ethnic Germans in a Slavic nation were subject to discrimination that, fanned by the actions of British intelligence, became flames of violence and ethnic anarchy. British agents, assisted by the Polish government, backed an anti-German Czech "nationalism" that included pogroms against German peasants and workers in the new German nation, as well as sabotage of German-language media and a concerted effort to destroy German culture.

Thus Hitler entered into the Sudentenland as a protector. When the Czech government refused to recognize and grant a plebiscite for the liberation of the Sudentenland, Hitler ordered his troops to occupy it, and, when British war mongering intensified, Hitler was forced to occupy the entirety of the Czech and Slovak nations and establish them as dependent client states. His intentions were clearly not to keep Czechoslovakia in a state of dependency, but to divide it, as it was divided in the 1990s, into two states, and to return the non-Czech and non-Slovak minorities to their own home countries. However, his intentions were never realized, as the British moved quickly to provoke World War II.

Having lost Czechoslovakia, the British had only one ally left to the east of Germany, and that was Poland. If they were to lose this, they knew they would lose all chance of encircling Germany in a future war—and encirclement was a major goal of British policy. The British were blinded to the way that the economic chaos and the continuous collapse of successive French government has eviscerated their ally in World War I, and could not understand that the Jewish government(s) of Leon Blum that had pursued a massive anti-militarist policy in France had made the idea of an encirclement of Germany impossible from the west. The British believed that the Polish, wielding horses and charging with swords drawn, could hold back the German tanks the way the French infantry had held back the German soldiers 20 years before, and were intent upon sustaining a hostile Polish presence on the German eastern flank.

The lands of northern Poland had vacillated between Teuton and Slav for 800 years, but had become a German heartland and had not been governed by a Slavic government for perhaps 500 years when they were suddenly transferred to the new Polish state in the wake of the Russian Revolution. Like the Sudentenland, they were inhabited by Germans who had been shorn from their Fatherland, and they rightfully belonged to the nation of the German people. Yet the Poles still remembered the deprivations they had suffered under the Teutonic Knights, and had conducted a campaign of revenge in their new German territories, fueled by the same nationalism that had sustained them against communism. The old rhetoric, spread by the Jews, of the incompatibility of the German and Slav, both Aryans and cousins in the Indo-European family, had sunk too deeply into the popular consciousness. Thus the Polish state was unable to act in the interests of its people and accept a compromise on the issue of renationalization of its German land. It had faith in the faithlessness of the capitalist Jews and it believed that Britain would appear and be its savior—and thus the spark was set for the second great conflagration.

Adolf Hitler did not believe himself to be the savior of Germany. He believed himself to be the one who was to lay the foundation for the appearance of the savior of the Indo-European world—the being that the Vedic Aryans had known as Kalki, the final avatar of Vishnu.

CHAPTER FIVE

THE WORLD AGAINST ITS SAVIOR

"**B**rother will fight brother and be his slayer . . . hard it is in the world . . . axe-age, sword-age, age of cloven shield, wind-age, wolf-age, as the world plunges headlong, no man will spare another."

So says the Voluspa, the prophecy of the seeress, in the Nordic Poetic Edda, telling of the end of the last age of the world. And so the world was witness in the midst of the 20th century as the forces of the demons of democracy, communism and Zionism allied themselves to destroy God incarnate as the savior of the world, Adolf Hitler.

The blow by blow of the war and its campaigns and its battles are of less importance than the meaning of the struggle of the allied forces of Masonic capitalism and democracy, Jewish Bolshevism and Jewish Zionism against the men who struggled to save the world and its peoples from the destruction and terror that these ideologies of hatred inevitably sought to impose. To see the struggle of capitalism and communism against National Socialism as a mere political struggle is to reduce the spiritual to the material, and to participate in the atheistic and false worldview of the Jewish powers. What occurred was a spiritual struggle of the same demonic forces of chaos which have threatened the world since the first pharaoh established the rule of Ma'at against Isfet in the Nile Valley against the same force of order represented by the Sun that rose and dried the waters to establish the Earth as a preserve against the ever encroaching threat of evil. Adolf Hitler was a god incarnate in the Aryan tradition, and while not the last incarnation of the god, he was another great avatar in the chain of avatars which laid the foundation for the final appearance of the god the Vedas knew as Vishnu.

As Savitri Devi teaches, Kalki—Vishnu's last avatar—is "the last incarnation of the divine sustainer of the universe and, at the same time, the destroyer of the whole world; the savior who will put an end to this present 'yuga' in a formidable display of unparalleled violence, in order that a new creation may flourish in the innocence and splendor of a new age of truth. In the Vedic triumvirate, Vishnu, the world-sustainer, is the tendency of every being to remain the same and to create (and procreate) in its own likeness . . . Shiva, the Destroyer, is the tendency of every being to change, to die to its present and to all its past aspects. He is Mahakala, time itself; time that drags the universe to its unavoidable doom and, beyond that, to no less irresistible regeneration." Yet, "Vishnu and Shiva, the world-sustainer and the world-destroyer, the force 'against time' and time itself . . . are one and the same. And they are also Brahma, timeless existence, the essence of all that is."

Thus the avatars that appear to allow the Aryan race to create and procreate, to grow and live, to expand, and to manifest in this world the beauty and love and life that is the divine order, are also the masters of destruction and death, and fulfill the divine duty of protecting and recreating the order that God has established in the world through the massive destruction of the inferior forms of life that the death-forces encourage, breed and manifest themselves in.

But there is no illusion that, before the final battle, that battle in which, the Voluspa tells us, "The Sun turns black, Earth sinks into the sea, the bright stars vanish from the sky, steam rises up in the conflagration, a high flame plays against heaven itself," the forces against time can be victorious. This doctrine as well known in the Nordic tradition as in the Indo-Iranian tradition of the Vedas, and was embodied in the West in the ideal of the *mors triumphalis*, or "triumphant death," which leads the warrior to Valhalla. As Julius Evola tells us in his *Metaphysics of War*:

"Valhalla, the seat of celestial immortality, [is] reserved for the 'free' divine stock and the heroes fallen on the battlefield. The lord of this symbolic seat, Odin or Wotan, appears in the Ynglingsaga as the one who, by his symbolic sacrifice on the 'world tree,' showed the heroes how to reach the divine sojourn, where they live eternally as on a bright peak, which remains in perpetual sunlight, above every cloud. . . . But this is not all. The spirits of the fallen heroes . . . add their forces to the phalanx of those who assist the 'celestial heroes' in fighting the Ragnarok, that is to say, the . . . 'darkening of the divines,' which . . . has threatened the world since time immemorial."

In other words, the sacrifice of the lives of perhaps 30 million people of German descent—perhaps 12 million of them in Germany proper—during World War II cannot be seen as a waste or mindless destruction of life, and the eternal Reich which those Germans who fought against the forces of the demons Baal, Seth and Apep, manifest in democracy, Zionism and communism, defended cannot be seen as destroyed or defeated in any meaningful sense, since the true empire which Adolf Hitler and his forces sought to defend was not the material empire of National Socialist Europe but the spiritual empire which is the natural inheritance of the Aryan peoples, and which exists on a divine plane that only at times chooses to become manifest in the material world. The sacrifice of the material forces of men in service of the Aryan ideal was necessary to bolster the spiritual forces of the great creator god which he will unleash at the end of the world. As the Bhagavad-Gita tells us:

"Killed you will attain heaven; victorious you will enjoy the Earth; arise, therefore, resolved to fight."

Evola's translation of the term Ragnarok as "darkening of the divines" is also significant, as it likely represents a better translation of the term "Ragnarok" than that typically given by Nordicists, who see it as a single day or a single battle in which the dusk of the powers occurs. Ragnarok is an ongoing process in which the divinity that once existed in men, and which was preserved in the Arya among the white race, is darkened and soiled by pollution from the spiritual elements which are manifest most directly in the Jewish people, as well as the collection of demonic forces and demon worshippers who choose to ally themselves with the Jew.

World War II was entirely the effort of the demonic forces of the material world to resist and to destroy the forces of a god that they know is doomed to destroy them and to utterly eradicate the decadent life that the Jews, their ideologies and the non-Jews who participate in the Jewish way of life represent.

In this context, the supposed heroism and the false honors that have been paid in both the United States and the Soviet Union to those now aging bacteria who served in the militaries of those countries during World War II must be examined. As Julius Evola notes, American and Soviet war veterans—those men who fought against god in the flesh in the person of Adolf Hitler—represent:

"[A] degraded warrior principle, which has passed into the service of hierarchically inferior elements . . . " whose warrior principle is "united . . . to an evocation and an eruption of instinctual, sub-personal, collective, irrational forces, so that there occurs, basically, a lesion and regression in the personality of the individual, who can only live life in a passive manner,

driven either by necessity or by the suggestive power of . . . pas-
sionate impulses," or, "human types who, driven to war by fake
idealisms, at last realize that reality is something very different
. . . all that impels them forward through the most terrible tests
is elemental forces, impulses, instincts and reactions, in which
there is not much human remaining, and which do not know
any moment of light."

Thus those who served the dark age and the demonic forces
of the Jew are denied Valhalla and the eternal life that ends in
resurrection at the time of the final battle. For them, war is a
dehumanizing experience that reduces them from their tenu-
ous hold to human-hood to the purely irrational and animal—
the spiritual condition upon which the demonic forces that
guide them depend on for the consumption of their souls.

With this spiritual understanding of World War II established, one can turn to the events of the war itself. The war was
instigated and initiated by Britain and France. The Poles, allies
of the British, launched a series of attacks on German civilians
in both Polish territory and across the border in Germany
proper, as part of a campaign of terrorism organized by the
British bankers and their mercantile state, and as part of a stated
Polish effort to expand its national territory to the Oder—a goal
which was achieved in postwar communist power brokering.
Speaking at the time of Poland's defeat, Hitler told the Reichstag that:

"Minorities in [Poland] suffer[ed] what amounted to a reign
of terror. I do not consider it my task to speak of the lot of the
Ukrainians or White Russian population, whose interests now
lie in the hands of Russia.

"However, I do feel it is my duty to speak of the lot of those
helpless thousands of Germans living in [Poland] . . . whom
the Poles now began to oppress and drive out. Since March,
1939, they had been victims of truly satanic terrorization. How

many had been abducted and where they are cannot be stated even today.

"Villages with hundreds of German inhabitants are now left without men because they all have been killed. In others, women were violated and murdered, girls and children outraged and killed. . . . Just as tens of thousands of Germans were slaughtered and sadistically tormented to death, so German soldiers captured in fighting were tortured and massacred."

And Hitler went on to discuss the 3,404 German soldiers, captured by the Poles, who were described as missing, but had largely been tortured and killed.

Such was the way that the allies of the British—the Polish government, which never commanded the loyalty of more than 15 percent of the Polish people—conducted their war, and it contrasted heavily with the humane restraint that characterized all of the efforts of German National Socialism on the battle-field. As Hitler stated in the same speech:

"Sheer sympathy for women and children caused me to make an offer to those in command of Warsaw at least to let civilian inhabitants leave the city. I declared a temporary armistice and safeguards necessary for evacuation. . . . I extended the time limit and ordered bombers and heavy artillery to attack only military objectives . . . I thereupon made an offer than the whole suburb of Praga [a suburb of Warsaw—Ed.] would not be bombed at all, but should be reserved for the civilian population in order to make it possible for them to take refuge there."

This restraint, which characterized all of Hitler's war policies, was the greatest weakness of the avatar as he went about his mission of eliminating the evil forces of cultural poison and pollution from decadent Europe. It was not his "racism," his "hatred" of non-Germanic or Slavic peoples, or his desire for "genocide," nor the alleged "brutality" of his war policies, but his love for his fellow man and his desire to protect non-combatants that characterized the German conduct of World War II at every turn. In comparison to the demonic forces that were arrayed against him, who committed actual acts of torture, cruelty and genocide at every turn, Hitler did everything within his power to prevent such actions. But, unlike the democracies, who murdered and tortured the best men and women of Europe while preaching a lying doctrine of peace, Hitler was frank about the violence that was needed to protect the great divine empire that had been entrusted to him by the Aryan gods. As Savitri Devi tells us:

"Evolution in time goes hand in hand not with a decrease in violence . . . but with a steady decrease in honesty regarding violence, and in understanding concerning the right use of it."

But despite the fact that World War II began with the destruction of the British puppet government in Poland, there should be no question that blame for the war itself lies wholly with the Judaized government of Britain, and the demonic, Masonic and Jewish financial interests that controlled it.

As Evola noted, "The center of the British empire lies . . . in the Jew and the Judaized Aryan [in which] the degenerate remains of a 'civilization of warriors' serve a 'civilization of merchants.'"

Or, as Devi tells us, "England's leading men . . . were not only short-sighted politicians but active agents of the everlasting dark forces." The British wanted to destroy Germany, nominally, because they still sought the ideal of economic domination of the world, and Germany had broken free from the system of international banks whose foundations the Jews had laid in Britain with the government of Cromwell and the later establishment of the Bank of England. But, metaphysically, the Masons and Jews which controlled the government of Britain wanted to destroy Germany because they recognized in the person of Adolf Hitler that god of light and life which they were sworn, by their oaths and initiation into the mysteries of the dark powers they served, to combat and destroy at every instance.

That Britain and its European allies were quickly and handily defeated should be no surprise. The government of Poland was in no way qualified to combat the superior military form of the German Reich. Polish independence had been largely the product of the combat of capitalism against the early stage of the Bolshevik Revolution—combat between the demonic powers over the corpse of the Europe they murdered in World War I—and Poland was an artificial state of the bourgeois-national type. France, similarly, had been hollowed out and prepared for defeat by the government of the Jew Leon Blum, whose socialist-communist forces had been struggling to disintegrate the French nation much the way their comrades in German had imposed decadence and weakness through the Weimar Republic. Britain itself was exposed in its decadence through its combat—its forces were routed at every turn, and the war it provoked quickly turned into a stalemate which time seemed to be ending in Germany's favor.

Hitler did not want this war, however, and the fact that Britain was not conquered by National Socialist forces is more the result of Hitler's excessive desire for peace with his racial brethren than any act or character of the British. That they endured the unnecessary deprivations of World War II without complaint is more indicative of the foolishness of the British people than their inner strength; that they allowed their government to massacre the innocent people of Germany their cowardice and inner weakness. The reason that, after the defeat of Poland and France, World War II largely stalemated was that Adolf Hitler wished to reach peace with Britain and not destroy its empire, which Hitler saw as an important structure for the maintenance of white and Aryan control of the peoples of the Third World. Hitler did not want a global German empire—he wanted a world under the control of the united forces of the European peoples, and their white race—and Britain was, for him, a key component of this future world peace.

In Britain, there were those who recognized the nature of the struggle and its potential consequences for both their nation and Europe. Hitler had warned Britain that "no matter what happens, England will be broken, one way or another," and Sir Oswald Mosley was the foremost among those British who predicted that a war of Britain against National Socialist Germany would end in the destruction of the British empire, even if Britain were to emerge victorious. In this, he was correct. Churchill knowingly bankrupted and exhausted Britain in a war he knew Britain could not win, except pyrrhicly, in conjunction with his allies, because, in his drunken stupor, he knew only that he must serve the dark forces with which he had forged his personal alliance.

Because Hitler hated war, after the destruction of the British puppets in Poland he struggled with Britain for peace. As Hitler himself said to the Reichstag, after the defeat of France:

"Now that peace . . . threatened to be crowned with success, the Jewish, capitalist warmongers, their hands stained with blood, saw their tangible pretext for realizing their diabolical plans vanish into thin air. Once again, we witness the conspiracy of wretched, corruptible, political creatures and money-grabbing financial magnates, for whom war was a welcome means of furthering their business ends. The poison scattered by the Jews throughout the nations began to exercise its disintegrating influence on sound common sense. Scribblers concentrated upon decrying honest men who wanted peace as weaklings and traitors, and upon denouncing the opposition parties as the 'fifth column,' thus breaking all resistance to their criminal war policy.

"Jews and Freemasons, armaments manufacturers and war

profiteers, international businessmen, stock exchange jobbers seized upon political hirelings of the desperado type who described war as something infinitely desirable."

But Hitler spent months struggling against this conspiracy within capitalism, and, with his newfound friend, Italy's Mussolini, whose nation had not yet entered the war, and whose government had been close to both Britain and France in the prewar period, he attempted to broker a peace agreement. But, as Hitler noted,

"It was only the Franco-British warmongers who desired war—not peace. More than that, as Mr. Chamberlain said, they needed a long war because they had now invested their capital in armament shares, had purchased machinery [for war], and required time for the development of their business interests [in the war industries]."

Further, Britain drew up plans for the invasion of Germany through the medium of one of the neutral countries on Germany's northern and northwestern frontiers. It was after the fall of Paris that the Germans captured documents proving British plans to invade Norway, Sweden, Denmark, the Netherlands and Belgium in order to attack the German homeland, but knowledge of these plans reached the German government in the early part of 1940—prompting the German campaigns which captured all of those countries except Sweden—whose neutrality German intervention in Norway happily preserved—and removed their pro-British governments. Though it is little known, the British had already begun their attack on Norway when the Germans invaded. British special forces units infiltrated Norway on the 5th and 6th of April 1940, three and four days before the German invasion of April 9th, and the main British force had planned to enter Norway on the 8th of April, and had been delayed only by poor weather. Similarly, in Belgium and Holland, it was the massing of British and French forces on the border of

France with Belgium on May the 6th and 7th, part of preparation for a campaign to invade those nations and establish a new front with Germany, that provoked the German response that ended with the capture of Paris and the fall of France.

During the French campaign, the characteristic mercy of Hitler in his treatment of the retreating British has been captured in the escape of the British army at Dunkirk. Though this army could not have withstood the Germans on any grounds, and never posed a serious threat to the German Reich at any point during the war, including the final campaigns, where it was bolstered by Soviet and American forces, the mercy and love for human life that Hitler showed in allowing Britain to withdraw from France has been characterized as Hitler's great "error" and a sign of his "erratic" or even drug-addled nature. In reality, it was one of the many overtures toward peace that Hitler pursued, even as his armies marched through the capitals of all of his European opponents. As Hitler himself stated:

"Responsible elements in Britain and France scented, in any appeal [for peace], a dangerous attack on their war profits. They therefore immediately began to declare that every thought of conciliation was out of the question, nay, even a crime, that the war had to be pursued in the name of civilization, of humanity, of happiness or progress, and, to leave no stone unturned, in the name of religion itself. . . . For if I had any justification in believing in victory, I should never have proposed an understanding with Britain and France without making any demands.

"In a very few days these agitators had succeeded in representing me to the rest of the world as a veritable coward. For this peace proposal of mine I was abused, and personally insulted. Mr. Chamberlain, in fact, spat upon me before the eyes of the world, and following the instructions of the instigators and warmongers in the background . . . declined to even mention peace, let alone to work for it. Thus the ultra-capitalist clique of people with a personal interest in the war clamored out for its continuance."

And, after the war, they have continued to clamor and justify it, in terror that the lies they have told about the conflict they began and the massacre of white European people that they instigated in service to their demonic gods will generally known.

By 1940, Britain was thoroughly defeated and incapable of mounting a meaningful offensive against German forces anywhere in the world. The Italian expeditions into north Africa ran across problems because the Italian military under Mussolini was incompetent and weak, and generally incapable of victory in any of its campaigns. In fact, with the exception of the drag that Mussolini's blundering in France, Africa and the Balkans was placing upon the German Reich, there was little hope for the British in their campaign to return Germany to its state of economic vassalage—until they persuaded the communist Jews of Russia to push their inhuman Bolshevik armies into the war in defense of British colonialism and global capitalism.

The Battle of Britain and the German bombardment of British cities constituted the next phase of the war, but it was a phase of the war which the British government, through its unyielding hatred and its desire to perpetuate war for the perpetuation of the profits of the little men its democracy had elected, brought upon its own people. Churchill began the campaign with the bombardment of German cities, and Hitler stated to his people in a speech announcing his campaigns against London and the other British cities:

"I waited for a month [after the fall of France], because I thought that after the conclusion of the campaign in France the British would give up this method of warfare [the bombing of German civilians]. I was mistaken. I waited for a second month and a third month. If bombs were to be dropped I could not assume the responsibility before the German people of allowing my own countrymen to be destroyed while sparing foreigners."

And thus Hitler was forced to order the mass bombing of British cities by the drunken warmongering hatred of Britain's own leaders.

Though the forces of capitalist Jewry and communist Jewry had engaged in nominal opposition to each other throughout the early part of the 20th century, and renewed that purely nominal opposition throughout most of the remainder, the two had never been truly enemies. The Jewish government which established itself in Russia in 1917—the government of Trotsky, Zinoviev and Kamenev—the government that consisted of more than 85% ethnic Jewish commissars, more than two-thirds of them of foreign—particularly American—origin—had been financed by a clique of Jewish bankers in Britain and America, most prominent among them Kuhn, Loeb and Company, and owed its existence to the international Jewish sense of solidarity. Thus, the alliance that was forged between the nominally capitalist British empire and the nominally communist empire of the Soviet Union is nowhere near as surprising or contradictory to the values of those nations as their surface level disagreement, designed to confuse the masses, would seem to represent.

That the Soviet Union was essentially an imperialist nation is so well recognized now that it is almost trite to repeat it, but even Stalin's establishment of the ideal of communism in one nation as the guiding principle of Soviet politics was more a concession to the reality of Soviet weakness vis-à-vis the capitalist nations rather than the abandonment of the struggle for a world Soviet empire. Like Hitler's National Socialist revolution in Germany, the communist revolution in the Soviet Union had needed time to consolidate itself and to transform the culture and the mentality of the people over which it governed. Unlike Hitler's government, the government of Stalin had had that time, and had produced, at the time it provoked war with Germany, a society capable—albeit through terror instead of by the German method of healthy and voluntary social unity—of producing a military machine that the capitalist nations could not defeat.

The Soviet purge of 1938 laid the basis for the production of a predominantly Jewish and communist officer corps, largely drawn from the political training schools of the Soviet government. And the peace that the Soviet Union had declared with Germany in 1939 was a concession to the need of the Soviets to train this new officer corps from the ranks of the party and the internal security forces. However, the peace of 1939 did not stop Soviet expansionism. The fact is that the Soviet Union had intended to expand upon other fronts and to allow the "crisis of capitalism" that it saw in the war between Britain and Germany to deplete its enemies before tackling Germany proper. First, the Soviets used the fixation of the West on their conflict with Germany to war with and win territorial concessions from Finland. It then took advantage of Germany's preoccupation with Britain and France to occupy the Baltic nations of Lithuania, Latvia and Estonia. Stalin also had expressed an intention to expand Soviet power in the Far East, particularly through communist revolution in China, as early as 1939, and in furtherance of this sought to limit the power of both the United States and Japan, preferably by provoking a war between the two—a situation which Soviet agents in the United States and their puppet Franklin D. Roosevelt managed to achieve on December 7, 1941.

In November 1940, Stalin had miscalculated that the time to risk war with Germany had come, and ordered Molotov to make a series of demands upon Hitler that could not have been met. Hitler had already been dragged into the Balkans by Mussolini's pre-emptive invasion of Greece, just ahead of the British forces that had been planning to occupy it, and Hitler had established and bolstered National Socialist governments in Hungary, Bulgaria and Romania. First, Molotov demanded concession in Romania beyond the territory of Bessarabia, which Hitler had advised Romania to cede to the Soviet Union. Second, Molotov demanded German support for a further Soviet invasion of Finland. Third, Molotov had stated that the Soviet Union intended to intervene in favor of communist forces in Bulgaria and wanted German guarantees of neutrality in such a struggle. Fourth, Molotov demanded German support for a Soviet sphere in Turkey, particularly a potential occupation of the Dardanelles to guarantee free access of the Soviet fleet to Mediterranean waters. There was also talk of the creation of a Soviet sphere in Sweden; again, the German war effort protected its Nordic northern neighbor. Concurrent with this, the Soviet government organized a communist-Serbian guerrilla force and began supplying weapons to support a communist uprising in the recently German occupied territories of the southwest Balkans. The German invasion of Serbia intercepted much of these armaments and smashed Russian plans for a front against Germany in the Balkans—but these Russian acts of aggression sealed the fate of tens of millions of the Russian people—and about 600,000 of its own Jewish commissars— as they forced Germany into war.

One of the strategic questions that had plagued the German Reich throughout the war was its lack of access to oil. Though efforts had been made to follow up the ill-conceived Italian invasion of northern Africa with a general penetration through to the Near and Middle Eastern oil fields, the ineptness of the Italian soldiery and the need for German troops in Europe had aborted this campaign. This left Germany dependent upon the government of Romania for oil—until the later effort to penetrate into the Caucasus—and, had Hitler agreed to let the anti-human forces of world communism expand into Bulgaria and Serbia, he would have been setting the stage for a communist coup in Romania that would have ended the German war effort through an end of its ability to fuel its tanks and fighting vehicles. Thus, Stalin knew that, even if Hitler had sought peace by any means, agreement to these demands would only have placed Germany in a weaker position when war with the Soviet Union inevitably came.

Concurrent with his demands, Stalin had also adopted an aggressive position on the German frontier. Of the 303 divisions possessed by the Soviet army, 258 were deployed in offensive positions against Germany in May of 1941, along with 15,000 of the 24,000 tanks the Soviets possessed, along with approximately 15,000 of the Soviet's 23,245 combat aircraft. This development was part of a Soviet strategy of aggressive war which it felt, by definition, was always a defensive war, as it was conducted in defense of the lumpenproletariat of the nation the Soviet Union chose to attack. According to Soviet military documents, Stalin had ordered by May of 1941 that Germany would be attacked no later than the spring of 1942.

Thus the myth of Hitler's "error" in "starting" a two-front war should be dispelled. Being the avatar of the Aryan god of order, Hitler's efforts were opposed by a world united in service to the demonic forces of death that had created, in the West, democracy, and, in the east, communism, to serve as two heads of the monster that sought, ultimately, to establish Zionism as the governing force over the entire Earth. Thus, these forces could not help but to assault Hitler's Germany at every turn, and it was only because of Hitler's great foresight that he was able to stay a step ahead of these forces of evil and aggression at almost every turn. As Devi tells us:

"The Fuehrer took on the terrible risk of a second front rather than become—and make the German people, in whose name he conducting the war—responsible for such an expansion of Soviet influence as, even after a complete German victory in the west, would automatically have placed half the world under the control of the mighty citadel of Marxism. . . . He knew also that a Russian alliance, sealed through his acceptance of the co-existence of a National Socialist Germany . . . and of a tremendous Marxist empire stretching from the Aegean Sea to the Bering Straits would be, in the long run, no guarantee against the absorption of Aryan man into that ugly, raceless and characterless sub-humanity, typical of this end of the Dark Age. . . . He knew that Marxism, and not the diluted and, moreover, obsolete forms of Jewish poison for Aryan consumption known as Christianity and Western democracy, is the final man-centered faith in the service of the dark forces; the doctrine destined to urge mankind to take the last step along the old way leading from primeval perfection to the fated depth of degeneracy, and, ultimately, to death."

On June 15, 1941, the Soviet Union ordered full mobilization on its front with Germany. Its intent was to break the German front in the south, through southern Poland and the Balkan nations, and to attempt to encircle German forces in East Prussia, where a defensive action would be fought along the German-Soviet border. Maps of German territory were transported to Soviet forces—an ironic move, as the same forces would lack maps of the Soviet territory through which they would soon retreat—and Stalin had already begun bolstering his military with the draft of 800,000 Russian militiamen and tens of thousands of technical specialists that had occurred in May 1941.

Though Germany vastly underestimated the military strength of the Soviet Union, they were aware of its efforts against the Reich. In June of 1941, Lt. Gen. Jodl and Field Marshal Keitel, two of the leaders of the German forces in the east, informed Hitler that the Soviet Union "was conducting the most gigantic military deployment in history, directed against Germany." While access to the Russian archives, after the Soviet collapse, has confirmed all of this, and the knowledge of Stalin's intentions is rather non-controversial in the United States, it is a testament to the strength of postwar communism in supposedly free Europe that early efforts to publicize the fact that Stalin, not Hitler, had provoked the conflict between German and the Soviet Union, and the Soviet units that were so thoroughly beaten by the Germans in the early stages of the war were hyper-prepared, not unprepared, for war with Germany.

Thus, on June 22, 1941, the die was cast, and German forces attacked Soviet communism, driving its armies in massive retreat across the entire front and liberating the eastern part of Europe from the terror of the Red Beast.

At this point, it is appropriate to address the question of alleged German atrocities—a series of fictions which were manufactured out of the whole cloth by the Jews of the Soviet Union and which were broadcast in the West solely through Jewish media organizations relying on the reports of their communist brethren. It should be stated unequivocally that the National Socialist government of Germany never engaged in an effort to exterminate the Jewish population of any nation—and that, in preserving these spawn of the demon Seth-Typhon, it likely erred.

Jewish atrocity propaganda against National Socialist Germany began upon the ascension of the Hitler government in 1933. Particularly, claims of mass extermination, mass arrest and persecution were directed against National Socialist Germany, and Jewish elements, particularly in the United States and Britain, declared "war" on Germany shortly after the National Socialists began to withdraw Germany from the world economic system that Britain and its capitalist Jews dominated. Until the German-Soviet alliance of 1939, these propaganda efforts were assisted by the Soviet Union, which resumed and intensified such propaganda after war between the two empires resumed in 1941.

However, it is widely recognized by mainstream historians that no atrocities against Jews *per se*, and no general persecution of the Jewish people, occurred prior to the outbreak of war in 1939. This position has been revised on several occasions, and Jewish propaganda organs in the United States remain free to broadcast all sorts of lies—usually in the form of personal anecdotes and accounts—that are not in accordance with the pseudo-"scholarly" view of this portion of history. However, according to the most recent revision of mainstream "holocaust" pseudo-scholarship, approximately 25,000 people were arrested in Germany between 1933 and 1939 and charged with political and social crimes. Of these, the average length of incarceration was six to 12 months, and the place of incarceration was almost always a minimum security prison camp comparable to the modern "Club Fed" minimum security institutions used in America for non-violent criminals today. There were 108 executions of criminals during this period, and those executed were generally executed for violent crimes that would have led to the death penalty in the United States both then and now, particularly murder. Few if any of those executed were Jews.

Yet Jews fled Germany during this period claiming persecution, largely because the anti-social activities that they had engaged in prior to the ascension of National Socialism, particularly the advocacy of communism, active treason against Germany in favor of the Soviet Union, the use of newspapers and university posts to promote the interests of foreign powers and anti-German forces, and the promotion of sexual crimes, particularly prostitution, pornography and abortion (all illegal in the United States during the same period), were no longer tolerated. In fact, it is estimated that two thirds of those who were imprisoned in Germany during the period 1933-1945 for political crimes, and who were released at the end of the war into the zone of control of the capitalists, were re-imprisoned by the occupying British, French and American forces between 1945 and 1948. Thus, Jews who proudly display the tattoos given them when they were admitted into German prisons should not be lauded as heroes, but should be asked what their crimes were, and made to admit that they were anti-social elements who deserved much worse than the extended vacation at the German "Club Feds."

This persecution, not of Jews, but of the crimes that were disproportionally committed by Jews, extended into the Soviet front, and it is the mass execution of communist commissars, who were overwhelmingly Jewish, and who had been responsible for war crimes and acts of genocide against the Russian people since their ascension to power in 1917, that forms the basis of the "holocaust" myth.

The Jews of the Soviet Union executed more than 25 million people during the period of 1917 through 1938, not including those killed in military conflicts associated with the civil war that followed the Bolshevik Revolution. Those they killed were often tortured or killed horribly—as many as 7 million were starved to death in Ukraine alone. Of the remainder, crucifixion of priests was a favorite tactic of the Soviet Jew, as well as the torture and slow murder of "reactionaries" in a process of lingering mutilation, amputation and castration that ended in the death of the "anti-Soviet element." Mass rape and sexual torture were components of the Jewish-Soviet system, and the Jewish people of the Soviet Union as a whole, as well as the Jews of America, Britain and the world who supported them, bear collective responsibility for the mass of bloodshed that was, in its essence, the sacrifice of the "best of the gentiles" that the Jewish Talmud demands in appeasement of the Jews' terrible god. These atrocities are so well documented that the space they deserve here, in contextualizing the so-called "holocaust," will be omitted, and the reader will be directed to the voluminous tomes written on the subject of communist and Soviet crimes against humanity instead.

It was because the Jews of the Soviet Union were so familiar with mass murder that they were able to attribute such acts to National Socialist Germany with such ease. And it was true that, where the National Socialists were able to capture Soviet commissars and political apparatchiks, they executed them—in just revenge for the 25 million these commissars had murdered. And it was also true that, among those executed for the crime of genocide against the peoples of the Soviet Union, and for the crime of the torture, rape and mutilation of their victims, were approximately 600,000 guilty, bloodstained Jews who had delighted in the prolonged death of those they had killed and received the lenient treatment of a short death from machine-gun fire or a bullet to the back of the head.

The Soviets knew that their agents in the mass torture and murder of mankind would receive no sympathy, and thus they were forced to create the myth of the extermination of civilian Jews in German-occupied territories. Their primary organ for this in the West was the publication *Soviet War News*, which was largely controlled by the Jewish Soviet leader Ilya Ehrenberg. Ehrenberg was an advocate of genocide who helped organize and orchestrate the massacre of German civilians after the war, and who had helped cover up the atrocities of the Soviet army during the war's early stages, particularly during the occupation of Poland. From *Soviet War News*, American newspapers and radio stations, many of which had been snatched up by the Jews during the Great Depression, broadcasted the lies of the Soviet empire to the people of the United States, talking of the alleged massacres that the Germans had committed against the

Jewish people. But it is now known that many of these alleged massacres—such as the alleged massacre of millions by "gas vans" that entered the public consciousness during the Soviet show trials of captured German officers in 1943, were complete fabrications.

Similarly complete in its fabrication was the myth that "six million" Jews were massacred during World War II. This myth first appeared in *Soviet War News* in early 1944, before the now advancing Soviet forces had entered German territory, and its author was the aforementioned Ehrenberg, who had fabricated the entire myth of the German "death camp" system. At the time, the center of these executions was alleged to be the German camp at Majdanek, though the center of these deaths was later moved to the camp at Auschwitz. Though German and Polish Jews never died on such a scale, the Soviets felt no restraint in conjuring any lie to justify their own policies of genocide against ethnic Germans in the territories they occupied—a campaign of genocide that would leave one-third of the German people of Europe dead.

And here it should be noted that these lies became so central to the war effort of not only the Soviets but their capitalist allies that, upon conclusion of the war, to justify the most horrendous waste of human and economic resources that the world had ever seen, these lies had to be continued and perpetuated— not only by the Jews who sought to exploit them for financial gain and to justify the Zionist occupation of Palestine, but by the gentiles who had allied with the Jews in their quest for the extermination of Germany. It was this need to justify the crime that was Allied aggression during World War II that led the Soviets to build the camp now shown to the world as Auschwitz, and now widely admitted to be a "reconstruction" undertaken by the communist Jews in 1948—not the original location of supposed "gassings" and "mass executions."

It should also be noted here that, while, in the immediate aftermath of the war, the Allies, particularly Americans, claimed to have "liberated" supposed "death camps," particularly Dachau, it is now admitted by mainstream pseudo-"scholars" that Dachau, and all of the other camps alleged by America and Britain to have been "death camps," were, in fact, merely prison camps, and no mass executions occurred there. The only alleged organized mass executions of civilians that occurred during the war occurred in territory that was later occupied by the Soviets, and the only evidence for such mass executions are Soviet "re-creations"—of buildings, of complexes and of documents.

Ultimately, the campaign against the Soviet Union was a failure, largely because the Soviet Union was too large and too underdeveloped to support the blitzkrieg tactics and advanced mobile infantry and armored force that the German army depended upon for victory. Further, Stalin was simply too ruthless, and he was willing to exterminate the entirety of the people under his rule in order to preserve his dictatorship and avoid responsibility for the crimes he had perpetrated against humanity. Though the Soviet army suffered 20 to one casualties against the Germans, and often were forced into battle with machine guns at their back by Soviet internal security units, they were able, in conjunction with the genocide of German civilians in the fatherland by Allied bombers and the mass destruction of the industry needed to support the German war efforts, to defeat the German forces and, eventually, win World War II.

But it is not widely admitted in America that it was the Soviet Union, and not the united forces of Britain and Germany, which conquered National Socialist Germany. Instead, the myth has been perpetrated that America "saved Europe" by launching the Normandy invasion at the last minute, just as Hitler was poised to achieve world domination. Of course, this is a lie. The British-American invasion of western Europe was designed more to prevent a complete domination of the European continent by Soviet communism than it was to smash the military power of Germany. In fact, without the defeat and massacre of the German army and German people on the eastern Front, the British forces, already defeated, even in conjunction with hordes of American-capitalist draftees, would not have been able to overcome the military force of the Reich. Even the beaten troops of Germany were able to mount a resistance the Americans and British could not break, and had the German officers not decided, in the final days of the war, that surrender to the forces of capitalism was a better alternative than eventual defeat by the forces of Soviet Jewry, the Americans and British would likely not have been able to secure as much territory as they did.

The only sphere in which America really contributed to a victory was in its immense grant of weapons and armaments to the Soviets, who had lost almost all of their ability to manufacture war materiel in the great German push against them of 1941. This loan of technology and war materiel, which laid a foundation for the technical parity of Soviet forces with their American counterparts in the Cold War period, and allowed the Soviet and communist assistance which defeated American forces in Korea and Vietnam during the Cold War, was decried at the time as "suicidal" by numerous American officials and scholars—officials and scholars who did not realize the extent of the penetration of the American government by communist-Jewish agents during the Cold War and the extent of the subservience of the Roosevelt government to its Soviet counterpart. As Devi tells us:

"No amount of manpower organized in a spirit of desperate resistance could have kept the German army from conquering Russia . . . had it not been for America's . . . direct and indirect help to the Communists; had it not been for the fantastic quantity of arms, ammunition and equipment that the USA sent over, in order to make the Russian . . . partisans increasingly dangerous and the Red Army irresistible; had it not been for an ever closer and more effective collaboration of the two sinister tools of World Jewry in the West—Roosevelt and Churchill—and of their misled people within the Marxist empire."

In fact, it was due to World War II that the supposedly "conservative" movement of the United States began to find what would become its defining alliance with the Trotskyite variant of communism—the ideological alliance that defines the modern Republican Party today. Stalin had purged Trotsky—one of his enemies with the good sense to flee rather than face torture and death—early in his career, along with many of the top Soviet Jews who could potentially have opposed him—and this purge had created an early split in international communism between Stalinists and World Jewry. This split intensified when Stalin made peace with Hitler. Those Jews, particularly in the United States, who had equivocated after the Stalin-Trotsky split, jumped the fence and allied themselves with a faction known in the United States as the Shachtmanites—named after Max Shachtman, the communist revolutionary who created the American neo-conservative movement. The later war between the Soviet Union and Germany did not bring them back into the fold—instead, they allied with American "conservative" elements, particularly William Buckley, and worked to redefine American conservatism as an instrument of world communism—a role that conservatives in the United States fulfill today.

The defeat of Germany in World War II was the beginning of the world cataclysm that has ended with the current state of being, with all of the Western nations dominated by Judaism in its various forms, both communist, Christian and conservative, and with those Western nations engaged in what is essentially a "mopping up" operation against the few remaining traditional cultures of the world, particularly the cultures of Islam.But the defeat of Germany did not represent the destruction of the Aryan ideal. While the Allies and the Soviets collaborated to kill perhaps 30 million of the 90 million people of Germanic ethnicity who resided in Europe prior to the war, they could not kill the collective spirit which those people represented. And while the defeat of Germany paved the war for the death forces to achieve world domination in the latter part of the 20th century, it has been known since ancient times that such domination and victory is a necessary precondition for the restoration of the original Golden Age of mankind. As Devi tells us, describing the last moments before Hitler's death: "The man against time . . . knew that his National Socialist wisdom, founded upon the very laws of Life; his wisdom that this doomed world had cursed and rejected, was, and would remain, in spite of all, as unassailable and everlasting as their everlasting dance."

Thus the futility of the efforts of the demonic forces of world destruction against the Arya is exposed, as such forces, lacking souls or spiritual depth, can only operate in the material world, and thus cannot touch the core of what they oppose, which is a divine force who, in eruptions such as that as Hitler and his Germany, is merely toying with his opponents, proving to them that, no matter how thorough their conquest appears to be, it is nothing but another act within a world governed by temporal principles that as inexorably lead toward their destruction as it inexorably guarantees their fleeting victory. At the moment that the last Aryan is sent to Valhalla, and the halls of Odin have finally reached their fill of the warriors that he has placed upon the Earth—at the moment of the supreme victory of the Jew and his forces of destruction over the remnants of the once greatest element of humanity—at that moment the skies will

open and the Jew and all of his peoples will be forever exterminated from the Earth. And thus, in the victory of the death principle, the death principle finds its own death, and Shiva the
Destroyer and Vishnu the Creator are united once again in
Brahma. The outward expression of the Aryan people can be
shattered, but the inner principle is immortal. As Evola taught:

"We will only recall that ancient Aryan humanity habitually
conceived of life as a perpetual battle between metaphysical powers, on the one hand the uranic forces of light and order, on the
other hand the dark forces of chaos and matter. This battle, for
the ancient Aryan, was fought and won both in the outer and
inner world. And it was the exterior battle which reflected the
battle to be fought within oneself, which considered as the only
truly just war: the battle against those forces and peoples of the
outer world which possessed the same character as the powers in
our inner being which must be placed under subjection and
domination until the accomplishment of a *pax triumphalis*."

Charles Manson became the idealized leader of a portion of the white liberation movement that gave up hope of ever reforming society. Yet Manson's cult of killer women was more a product of the drugs and decadence
of the 1960s than a model for revolution against the antifa political system.

CHAPTER SIX

THE CIVIL RIGHTS ERROR

I t was in the postwar period, between the destruction of National Socialist Germany and the destruction of the Soviet Union, that the Jews cemented their control over the culture of the West and sank their claws so deeply into America, the nation whose empire they had chosen to replace Britain's, that they could not be extricated. Once a potentially dangerous independent entity in a system controlled by Jewish-British finance, America became the center of the world revolution that the Jews of capitalism had chosen to replace their failed system of explicitly communist upheaval, and the American people became the bastardized slaves of the power that superseded and eventually replaced communism and capitalism —world Zionism.

World War II ended with the destruction of Germany and central Europe and the extermination of one-third of the ethnically German people of Europe. Prior to the war the number of ethnic Germans in Europe had numbered over 90 million; after five years of starvation by the Allies and torture and murder by the Soviets, that number had been reduced to just over 60 million, who, instead of being spread across the continent, were now herded into the rump elements that were allowed to retain the German name. The German people would take 50 years to recover the loss of their race and restore themselves to the mere number they possessed before the Jewish campaign of genocide against them, and it was only with the literal extermination of the German people that the National Socialist ideal they represented and carried within them was, for the moment, suppressed.

The defeat of Germany, though, was transformed by the lies of the Soviets and of their allies in Western Jewry into a moral parable, and this moral parable became the defining ideology of the post-communist "democratic" world that afflicts the planet today. The lie of the holocaust, and the attribution of genocide to Germany as a uniquely German phenomenon was used to obscure the crimes of the Jews that had been committed in the name of communism, and the communist movement to destroy the world was given new empowerment by unity with the idea of "love"—a "love" so all-encompassing that it not only embraced the lowest elements of humanity, but encouraged them to murder their betters. This "love" would find its ultimate expression in America in two peculiar ways—one, in the "hippie" movement that disintegrated white civilization during the Civil Rights Error and the ideology of "drugs, death and the devil" that gave birth to the Church of Satan, and, two, in the reaction to that among Christians which equally claimed and abused the notion of "love" in furtherance of the idea of Judaized Christian Zionism.

In the Jewish mindset, it is a "fact"—because the Jews declare it to be so—that all men are equal, though this "equality" is not only not real, but also irrational, and thus held to be merely an "ideal" that all men should strive toward. That the irrational and impossible can never be "ideal," as true ideals must be rooted in human experience and human possibilities and potentialities, is an idea alien to the Jewish mind state, which, being purely material and having no positive spiritual component, can conceive of ideals only as irrational abstractions without basis in reality. True ideals are the unique province of those who have connection to the spiritual realm and the higher functions of the soul. But the spiritually blind Jews are unable to recognize their own disability, and thus proceed forward with a kind of mockery of the ideal that can only be the perspective of a complete outsider to the spiritual and transcendent.

Because it is a "fact" that all men are equal—just as it is a "fact" that all races are equal, even though that, too, is obviously untrue, not only from the perspective of modern genetic science, but also from the perspective of common observation—anyone who diverges from that perspective must not be motivated by any rational thought or analytical feeling, but must be blindly pursuing "hate"—that boogeyman of the Jewish world that is feared precisely because it too accurately captures what the Jews themselves bear against the rest of the human world. So, if a person notices a correlation between behavior and race, or between behavior and consequences of behavior, and that these behaviors are at the root of human social equality and human differentiation, that person becomes labeled an irrational "hater," opposed to the religion of "love" preached by Jesus, who, as a rabbi, was and is a representative of the Jewish people. Or, equally, that "hater" is separated from the secular masses who understand the centrality of the principle of "mankind" that has been expressed so eloquently in the institutions of liberal democracy, and whose inequality is merely an artificial product of the desire of one group of "haters" to establish inequitable economic relations with another. Thus any connection to the real world, or any ability not to participate in the collective Jewish fantasy, is actually the product of a chthonic emotional retardation that must either be "educated" out of an individual or end in the individual's extermination—all in the name of "love."

In this context the philosophy of murder that is the heart of communism must be seen at the heart of the American civil rights movement and the various movements, including the movements for feminism, pacifism, homosexuality and drug addiction, that accompanied it. All were and are efforts to exterminate through violence the best elements of the non-Jewish peoples and to reduce non-Jewish people to an undifferentiated mud race that is genetically programmed to be the slaves of the Jews; in other words, like democracy and communism, the various movements for "love" and "equality" that dominated the postwar period and which continue to poison and pollute human society are just further steps in the ascension to world domination of a group of ancient demonic deities that desire to enslave and consume humankind.

The most obvious element of this movement is the practice of ritual human sacrifice which has become institutionalized under pseudo-scientific and pseudo-medical jargon as "abortion." Just as the Carthaginians sacrificed their children to Baal Hammon, and just as the ancient Jews sacrificed the best of the children of the non-Jews they captured to their god Yahweh, the Jews today murder several million human infants annually as part of a blood sacrifice that they believe empowers the demonic and imprisoned gods that are at the heart of their people's form of worship. It is well known in the Aryan Traditions, from that of the Classical world to the Vedic and the Nordic, that, when the Aryan sky-god, whether Zeus or Odin or Tyr, defeated the serpent being that rebelled against him, he was unable to destroy the serpent, but, instead, trapped it under the ocean and threw upon it an island to pin it there until the end of the world. Whether Typhon trapped under Sicily and Mount Etna, or Loki trapped in the cave under Hvergelmir, or the serpent Vritra trapped under the ocean by Indra, this being is still alive, and is waiting until the end of the world to escape and to lead the armies of the death forces against the host that will emerge from the heavens to destroy them. The belief embodied in the practice of ritual human sacrifice is that the blood—and often the flesh—of these victims is poured into the earth to give sustenance to this demonic being (or those beings who form his near associates). And it is the desire to feed and to give sustenance to the demonic powers which threaten the Earth that is the root cause of the Jewish desire to see millions of children murdered in the ritual of abortion.

But abortion is only part of the larger complex of the destruction and degradation of human life that accompanied the postwar crusades led by the Jews against the antiquated revolutionary form of democracy and in favor of the new revolutionary forms of communism and, more and more explicitly, Zionism and Jewish racial control. Beginning with the principle of "love," these forms inevitably end in degradation and murder, and the destruction of life and the higher aspects of living in favor of the continuance of mere biological existence by beings incapable of spiritual existence.

In the first chapter of this work, the differentiated origins of human beings were discussed, and it was shown that the white race likely represents a genetic development from the Neanderthal, as the Oriental race represents a development from *Homo erectus*, and the Negro represents a semi-human development from the degenerate form of Australopithecus, a pre-human type of ape-man. Alternatively, the Negro can be seen as a degeneration of the divine type—as man-like being which was unable to develop his potential into full participation in humanity, particularly because of his inability to develop a soul. Regardless, to assert the equality of the Negro, or any race bred with it, with the base material component of the Arya is *prima facie* nonsense, and occurs in our society only because of the force used by the Jews and their government to preserve official ignorance—much as the Catholic Church for centuries burned those who proclaimed the obvious truth, known to the ancient world, that the Earth revolved around the Sun.

The general inferiority of the biological material of the Negro does not imply the individual inferiority of the Negro to every person of white pigmentation that he encounters. Every race produces its degenerates and bastards, and the white race certainly produces its share of defects. In fact, as discussed, the Arya represents only a divine minority which uses the biological material provided by white people to manifest themselves in this world; they are not the race in its entirety. What differentiates the Negro and the white races is the ideal to which the Negro type strives to conform is inferior to the ideal to which the white race naturally attempts to conform, and this inferiority is manifest in the inability of the Negro to manifest or maintain culture or civilization in any form without the assistance, tutelage and guidance of the white race. A proof of this proposition is not needed here. Any student of history—or of the situation prevailing in those American cities which have fallen victim to democratic Negro government—can see its truth, and those who cannot fail to do so not because of the lack of evidence, but because of their willful decision to be blind to the obvious that is lying before their eyes. Really, the argument for Negro equality is so foolish that it does not deserve any answer but contempt, and the fact that it even has to be addressed is symptomatic of the depths of ignorance, superstition and depravity to which modern society has sunk.

The lesson, though, that the Jews taught America to glean from World War II was the inherent "evil" of any ideology that asserts racial differentiation, as the Jews asserted that it was the ideology of racial differentiation, and not the evil actions of their people against the German people, that was the root cause

of the war. To a people who barely understood what they had
fought against, and why they had slaughtered so many of the
best of the human race, this explanation satisfied an inner need
that obvious falsehoods—such as the alleged threat of invasion
that Germany had posed to the United States—could not. Few
of the American soldiers who had fought against the empire of
God had the inner fortitude and courage necessary to admit
the evil that they had participated in. There is an inner need of
men to feel that they have participated in and done something
good, even when the evil of their actions is before their eyes.
And as alcohol has always accompanied the atrocities of the
soldier, and marijuana would dim the memories of those who
committed the atrocities of the Vietnamese War, the drug of
holocaust propaganda and anti-authoritarian critique was used
to dope the memories of the American servicemen who had
participated in the Jewish crusade for evil.

Yet the lessons of World War II that the Jews sought to teach
America had substantial implications for American politics. The
communists in America had, early on, abandoned the class
struggle in favor of the racial struggle, and saw the instigation
of black revolution against America's white population as a
means of dividing the country sufficiently to establish Jewish
political, economic and cultural control. This tactic, furthered
by the Christian churches that had been established by Masonic
elements within Protestantism, had successfully broken America during the Civil War, and the Jews believed that these tactics
could be used to break America again.

Thus, ironically, as America engaged in a world conflict
against the Soviet Union and world communism, it became
communized and emerged from the Cold War as a more dangerous revolutionary and anti-human force than the naked evil
of Bolshevism itself.

The essential evil of civil rights and flower power can be divided into the several categories under which it chose to manifest itself. First, there was the movement for women's "rights," which particularly included the right to the ritual human sacrifice of unborn children to demons, aka "abortion rights," discussed above; second, the movement for "sexual liberation," which is broad enough to include the feminist movement, but also involved the legitimization of sexual exploitation, pornography, interracial sex, homosexual sex and other acts; third, the movements around racial issues, civil rights, desegregation, affirmative action, and the like; fourth, the movement to open borders to human traffic and to capital, known as immigration rights, trade rights, free trade, and the like; fifth, the movement to legitimize and mainstream the use of drugs; sixth, the "peace" movement. All of these movements tie in together and were the product of the same group of demonic activists working in conjunction to break down human society and destroy the human race, but can be divided because they are the many heads that the hydra of the Jewish serpent chose to show.

That "women's rights" was and is essentially a communist and Jewish production is undeniable to any woman who has been involved in feminism, and the names Gloria Steinem and Betty Freidan, among the many, many other communist Jews who led and organized the so-called "women's rights movement," should be enough to at least intrigue a reader unfamiliar with the question into reading more. "Women's rights" is a vague term and encompasses attacks on the human social order on many levels. As we have seen, it began with the radical communism of the late 19th century and ended with the ritual murder of more than a million children each year and the consumption of their blood, bodies and souls by the evil gods that have plagued mankind since the inception of the race. In between, it involved an attack, primarily within white communities, on the notion of masculinity, and on the traditional social roles of men, including their role in defending society. By encouraging women to revolt as women against an allegedly "male-dominated" society, the Jews and their cohorts worked between the sexes in the same manner they had worked between the races and between the classes of the human society they had pledged their souls to destroy.

The essence of all Jewish and Masonic liberalism is so-called "individualism," which, as the philosopher Julius Evola has noted, is, in the modern context, not the development of the individual to the highest potential, but the division of the individual from the society in which he finds context and meaning—what Evola calls "individuation." In a Traditional world, because all people cannot play all roles—not everyone is suited to be a president or a congressman, even if they can, just as not everyone is suited to be a billionaire—each person is encouraged to play the role in society that is best for them: the worker is encouraged to work, the merchant to trade, the warrior to fight, the governing class to rule. This is what Evola calls the positive freedom of Traditional society, where the social institutions assist the individual in realizing their inner being by assisting them in fulfilling their social role. In contrast, Judaized liberalism offers individuals only a negative freedom. The individual is not encouraged or assisted in being anything—instead, they are simply set free from the social bonds that would normally guide their life, and allowed to drift under the illusion that they can be "anything." Thus, by allowing the individual to be "anything," modern society guarantees that most individuals are nothing, which is all they are capable of being without the assistance of others. Thus welfare, unemployment and poverty are a guaranteed product of modern society.

The goal of the Judaized "civil rights" movement was to destroy all institutions that assisted the individual in being anything more than the nothing that the individual becomes when he is divorced from society, by falsely claiming that the guidance and assistance that society provided the individual were, in fact, restrictions on the individual's "freedom." This is the ultimate goal of the leveling movement that prophecy says will hasten in the reign of slave states on earth, just prior to the final death of mankind. By destroying the socio-cultural organisms that sustain human life, the Jew, like the Ebola virus in the human body, causes human society to liquidate, disintegrate into its parts and die.

With feminism comes "sexual liberation." The morals of the antiquated forms of Jewish subversion—the extreme denial of sexuality that comes with Christianity, for instance—was and is certainly pathological, but the healthy regulation of sexual impulses and the ability of the human race to respond to perversion of those impulses was and is not. Certain types of sexual behavior are discriminated against because they are harmful to human society or reflective of individual dysfunction. Mental problems often manifest themselves in violent and sexual behavior, and the human race is attuned to disabled and dangerous behavior in others—it is part of the ingrained survival mechanisms by which the individual preserves himself. Thus, homosexuality is not "sinful" or some offense against God—it is looked down upon by normal human beings because it is indicative of mental disorder and potentially dangerous or erratic behavior on behalf of the homosexual. The fact that homosexuals are disproportionately black (or, rather, the black population is disproportionately homosexual or bisexual, particularly among its males), poor, ignorant, criminal and mentally ill—not the gentile high fashion Jews or whites that they appear to be on TV and in Jewish media products—in other words, the fact that homosexuality—and other sexual perversions—tend to accompany dangerous dysfunction is the reason it is discriminated against. Similarly, incest and pedophilia tend to cause dysfunction in their victims, thus they are discriminated against. Other perversions also tend to indicate more general dysfunction—and, while there is no need to ban certain sexual acts that are only harmful to the already damaged individuals who participate in them, the movement for sexual liberation went further and demanded that the government eliminate the social stigma attached to such acts—by harming and persecuting those that denounced them. This kind of action—violence against the "best of the Gentiles" and those who would defend human society against the Jew—was the real aim of the movement for sexual liberation.

The other aim was to degrade women and to destroy the normal sexual relationships that are at the heart of familial relationships. Men and women were told that the restrictions society placed upon their sexual behavior were "repressive," and they were encouraged to act outside those restrictions. What resulted was that men and women discovered that one can rationalize any lie, but one cannot get around human nature —their relationships, their marriages, and their ability to raise children disintegrated as they became more "free" in their relationships—thus, their ability to be happy within a sexual relationship decreased as their "freedom" increased. Women ended up degraded—as women who are passed around by men always become degraded, whether philosophy says that is "sexist" or not—and ended up in relationships, at the lowest levels, with men who encouraged them to take up with other men in order to bring in money—the pimp-whore relationship that was the norm in Negro communities prior to the Civil Rights Error. They were also encouraged to degrade themselves by ignoring the racial and social barriers that would have made them avoid spiritually and genetically inferior men and the abusive relationships that derive from such men—and thus white women miscegenated with blacks and found that their race did not want them back when they were done. Again, despite the "racist" and "sexist" nature of such things, such women became and remain pariahs, outside of human society despite that society's formal and nominal "acceptance" and encouragement of their behavior.

And it should be no surprise that the sexual liberation movement, like the feminist movement, found its origins in the same discredited Jewish pseudo-intellectualism that we discussed in the entry to the 20th century. Franz Boas and Sigmund Freud were the two leading advocates of sexual liberation, Boas primarily through his student, the white woman Margaret Mead. Mead, for instance, published a work on tribes in Samoa claiming that their open sexuality would benefit modern society—decades later, it was proven that she falsified her data to draw a politically motivated conclusion. Freud was already coming into disrepute in the 1960s, but his writings helped spark the movement to "de-analize" society with sexual openness—a movement that Freud himself described as a "disease not a cure" during one of the frequent sessions where he boasted about the destructive nature of his teachings. While both the anti-racial anthropology of Franz Boas, which claimed there were no broad genetic differences among the races, and the sexual psychology of Sigmund Freud, which claimed sex was the basic drive behind human society, have been discredited and are no longer considered legitimate even by mainstream scholars, both were able to lie just long enough to achieve their goals of cultural poisoning and social distortion.

"Civil rights," desegregation and the like were likewise Jewish productions, though Negro front men often played a role, just as all instances of Negro "success" are generally the product of "unfair"—at least, non-meritorious, promotion by Jewish elements. The NAACP, for instance, was operated from its conception until 1975, by which time it had exhausted its role, by a series of Jewish presidents, most notably Arthur Spingarn, his brother Joel Spingarn and Kivie Kaplan, who led the organization during the Civil Rights Error. While the NAACP always provided a Negro front man for the TV camera, to make it appear that it was a "black" organization, it was likewise always almost entirely Jewish in its financing and organization.

Similarly, the black "radical" groups of the 1960s and 1970s, which were discarded and destroyed by their backers after they had served their purposes, were the products of Jewish radicalism and communism. David Horowitz, the racist anti-white Jew turned racist "pro-white" Jew, is perhaps the best known Hebrew organizer of the Black Panthers, but Huey Newton and Bobby Seale and their like came to their position of notoriety because of Jewish money and Jewish backers who organized and financed them and showed them how to structure their organization. After the destruction of the Black Panther Party, Bobby Seale—as an example known personally, at one point, to the author—was given a comfortable job in a university by these same Jewish backers—just as other pseudo-"black" radicals, like Angela Davis, were protected and promoted by the Jewish system which created them. That these "black" radical groups worked with other Jews, such as Jerry Rubin and Abbie Hoffmann, the Jewish founders of the Yippies who later secured comfortable stock exchange jobs, or Dana Beal, the publisher of the newspaper *Overthrow* who is now a radical and prominent New York Zionist, is just part of the same issue—the total control of "black power" by Jewish communism.

Thus the "freedom riders" who rode buses through the South and the "voting rights" activists who fought for "desegregation" were not "average Americans" or even average "college students," they were Jewish radicals who were working, in concert with more mature Jewish interests, to destabilize and destroy non-Jewish human society. Because they had big money behind them, they were able to buy most of the white Southern aristocracy, who had been raised to hate and exploit "white trash" and not give a damn about their lesser racial brethren, and eventually control the Democratic Party, as they do today. When the Southern white leadership learned that Jewish money would help them win elections without the support of poor white voters, they abandoned the white man they had supported with segregation and turned on him like the parasites the mercantile class, when not restrained by proper social institutions, always show themselves to be. The fact that Scottish Rite Freemasonry is rampant among these nominally white parasites should be of no surprise as well.

This move to "desegregate" the United States also has to be understood in terms of the wider move by the Jews and their gentile allies to massacre and commit genocide against white people worldwide in the same period. Particularly, the bloody war of extermination that was fought against white colonists throughout Africa, and particularly in Rhodesia and South Africa, should be a lesson to the whites of the United States today, just as the Haitian revolution should have been a lesson to them. The African National Congress of Nelson Mandela and Thabo Mbeki was, like the American NAACP, an almost entirely Jewish institution. Its founding members were Abbie Sachs and Yossel Slovo, and, like Roy Wilkins in the United States, its figureheads like Mandela and Mbeki were never more than mere front men. Similarly, the ZANU-PF of Rhodesia was almost the singular creation of Nicholas van Hoogstraaten, a Jewish financier in Britain who hated the indigenous white peoples of southern Africa, and who made huge profits speculating on war-impacted African real estate. While the Soviet Union outright financed these groups, support for them was won among the Western establishment because of the anti-

British nature of the Boers who seized control of the government of South Africa in the 1960s. The same Anglo-elite who created, with the Jews, the modern banking system, still held to the pre-World-War-II mentality of crushing any economic dissent, not realizing that their own efforts against ethnicities or divisions within their own race was allowing the serpent children of Typhon to seize global control. Whether they realize it now that their element of the white race has been largely supplanted even within their own citadels of power—such as the White House and the Pentagon—is questionable. These are people destined to die, spiritually and collectively, in pursuit of worthless paper money.

With the movement to "liberate" Negroes within the United States from the "bonds" that had forced them to hold jobs and produce and to play the limited useful role in society which their race is capable of, came the movement to "liberate" other peoples of the Third World, particularly by importing them into the United States to further muddy the racial waters and divide the American section of the white race. That this movement to "open borders," primarily to Mexican and Central American mestizos, was linked to the movement to open those same borders to international capital should come as no surprise.

With the "liberation" of the Third World colonies that had once belonged to the Western nations came a new form of exploitation in the form of international debt, as the plan of the "*London Times* set" to transition the British empire into a Commonwealth of nominally independent states came to fruition—but with the difference that the British were no longer operating those colonies; these new states became colonies of the Jewish international banking establishment. But in the developed Western nations, particularly those that had not been integrated into the British-Jewish banking system before the war, a new type of crisis had to be initiated to bring their economies down and into the international system—and the importation of the poverty of the non-white, non-Western world, combined with the exportation of the productive aspects of the economy, would be that mechanism, and this form of economic rapine would be the defining element of the post-Civil Rights, "conservative" and capitalist segment of the move toward New World Order.

The fifth leg of the Civil Rights Error assault on American society and culture was the spread of drugs and intoxicants, which reached an unprecedented level during the 1960s and which has continued to be a major destabilizing factor in American society and culture into the present time. Troubles with widespread use of intoxicants began in the 19th century with the expansion of the use of opiates within the British empire, and alcoholism has been a persistent issue fueling criminal acts in Western nations for time immemorial—but the use of hallucinogens, amphetamines, and, particularly, cocaine and its derivatives in the postwar period reached levels unprecedented in human history—and it is difficult to say this was the result of some accident or happenstance of human development. One element in the expansion of drug abuse was the efforts of the American CIA—a creation of World War II—to neutralize communist guerrilla movements in Latin America by turning them toward criminal activity—a stated tactic still taught in the American military's anti-guerrilla programs. Heroin manufacture was encouraged by the CIA in Central Asia, particularly during the 1970s and 1980s, as part of an effort to fund anticommunist guerrillas resisting Soviet expansion in that region—and most notably the Soviet invasion of Afghanistan. Notably, heroin use in the United States has fluctuated largely with the need for the CIA to finance criminal organizations in Central Asia, just as cocaine use has fluctuated with CIA involvement in South and Latin America.

That the CIA was involved in such campaigns is beyond denial. It has been exposed in the American press and this author
has personally known individuals, employed by the CIA or U.S.
Army, who were involved in the creation of the crack cocaine
distribution networks that the CIA created in the early 1980s to
finance the anti-communist movement in Nicaragua. However,
the use of these illegal drug networks during the 1950s, 1960s
and 1970s in the context of the Soviet-funded Jewish communist movements only found a nexus with the activities of the
American intelligence establishment. Like all efforts to weaken
their most powerful opponent, the Soviets saw the spread of
drug abuse among the American intelligentsia as necessary
component in the division and atomization of American society, part of general poisoning and weakening intended to pre-
pare the United States for invasion.

The impact of drugs upon the shaping of public consciousness through the Jewish owned media should also not be dis-
counted, as there is no question that many of the reporters who
were actively supporting the Soviet and Jewish efforts to destabilize the United States were manufacturing news out of whole
cloth based upon drug-induced fantasy. This author was once
employed by a man who worked as a personal assistant to *Washington Post* publisher Katherine Graham, a half-Jewish woman
descended from Eugene Meyer, the Jew who bought the paper
during the Depression, and the Graham family, which had
owned the paper historically. One of this man's jobs during the
late 1960s and 1970s was to courier drugs to *Washington Post* reporters who were using them while manufacturing political
news, particularly news during the collapse of the Nixon administration. That the people chosen to shape American culture
were largely addicts that were controlled and manipulated not
only by bad ideology but chemical dependence is a given.

Further, conservative elements were roped in, particularly

during the 1980s, into allowing and encouraging the spread of drug abuse in the United States in order to neutralize the left-wing resistance movements that had originally encouraged drugs to break down conservative American society. Just as the United States had neutralized guerrilla movements in Latin and South America by turning them toward criminal activities, black street gangs that had been politicized were turned toward crack cocaine distribution in order to eliminate their political element and cause them to focus upon illegal economic activities.

Thus, as we shall see, the mis-perceived interests of American intelligence and law enforcement and their "conservative" controllers converged with and complemented the efforts of the anti-democratic forces who were trying to overturn the now outdated form of revolution that had created America and bring it into the essentially communist and post-communist New World Order.

The sixth arm of attack that the Civil Rights Error used to infiltrate and subvert American society was the anti-war movement, just as the pro-war movement was used to infiltrate and subvert American conservatism. The Soviet Union was founded as a vehicle for world revolution, and it was used, as we have discussed, to overturn the monarchies of eastern Europe and to subvert the underdeveloped "Second World" nations that never experienced the democratic revolutions that began the collapse of Western civilization. Despite Stalin's nominal adherence to the principle of "socialism in one nation," the Soviet Union, and, later, Communist China, worked to spread revolution throughout the world, financing not only resistance movements within the United States, but armed guerrilla movements throughout the former colonies of the Western nations, and within the western European nations themselves.

Particularly ripe for such revolutions were the incredibly poor and overpopulated nations of eastern Asia, who had been conquered and subjugated by the Japanese empire prior to World War II, and by the British and French empires beforehand. Newly independent, and with their ethnic and cultural traditions shattered, these nations were easily suckered into anti-colonialist rhetoric—the kind of anti-colonialist rhetoric that Mao so successfully turned into the communist doctrine of Third World Nationalism—the idea that national revolution among non-white peoples is a predecessor or early stage of communist revolution. Further, Communist China had large masses of people that it could not effectively employ, despite the vicious "reforms," characterized by mass murder, that it was enacting in an effort to modernize its economy. It also needed something to do with its economy, and the production of cheap weapons and equipment for export or use has always been a road to economic recovery for an underdeveloped or underemployed nation.

Thus the Chinese, often with the assistance or at least moral support of the Soviets, pushed their communist allies in the Korean peninsula and southeast Asia into war.

That communism had to be resisted was unquestionable. The danger that world communism posed—and still poses—to the white race and its western nations was unquestionable. Yet those Western nations were merely subject to another, more primitive form of the revolutionary impulse that defines world communism, and the American establishment that was fighting for "democracy" could never truly or finally resist communism, as communism was merely an extension of the principles upon which the Masonic-democratic revolutions of the 18th and 19th century had been founded. Thus, no real resistance to world communism was possible as long as America remained an essentially internationalist and capitalist nation—and thus the wars that America fought to constrain communism were doomed to be themselves subsumed in the international shift toward a post-communist New World Order.

In the United States, opposition to the war was financed by the same foreign powers who were at war with the United States, while at the same time being rooted in a sensible American opposition to the creation of an establishment that was itself destined to doom America. By the end of the Cold War period, the demand for war against communism had itself become a subversive doctrine demanding war for a kind of democracy that was the same cultural subversion under a different name—and this transformation was due to the infiltration of the American "conservative" establishment by the Shachtmanite/Trotskyite "neo-conservative" revolutionaries whose rise we have previously discussed.

Thus, by the end of the Civil Rights Error, the principles of "anti-fascism" and the anti-National-Socialist rhetoric and lies that the United States had employed in its war against Germany were used as the foundation upon which largely Soviet and Jewish financed interests were able to build an edifice of cultural subversion, atomizing and individualizing the American people, breaking down the cultural organism that had united them, and, ultimately, gaining control of all of the remaining power centers within American society, maintaining nominal rhetorical differences, but so transforming those institutions that those which had tried to maintain a resistance to world subversion had become vehicles by which the world subverters were able to move forward toward their goals.

That resistance to these movements in the United States and abroad was so ineffectual would be a wonder, if the efforts of the nominally "conservative" forces, who had dedicated themselves to their own ineffectual and ultimately subverted forms of resistance, were not considered. Certainly, the United States that emerged from World War II in the 1940s did not want desegregation, anti-racism, homosexual rights, sexual division, drug abuse and social decay, and there was widespread and popular resistance to these efforts—widespread and popular resistance that was ultimately destroyed by the American intelligence and law enforcement establishments.

A key error in these resistance movements was their belief in legality and their desire to effect change within the context of American law and American political institutions. Such change, of course, was impossible, as the philosopher Max Stirner has noted, because all systems of law created by men are essentially systems designed to sustain and promote the interests that had created them, and thus any nominal change these systems allow is simply that—nominal and designed to misdirect and defuse effective forms of resistance. By deceiving the people into believing that democratic change is possible—and that only democratic forms of change are legitimate—the system is able to neutralize its opponents by channeling them into a system of legality that is designed to defuse them and make them ineffectual.

The Federal Bureau of Investigation, half of the government's mechanism of social control, was created in the prewar era, but World War II allowed it to greatly expand its capacities to monitor and control American dissent. With it, the Central Intelligence Agency—the organization most responsible for the current American drug problem—was created during World War II, and, due to the admitted intense interaction between foreign and domestic political subversion, quickly expanded its activities against American citizens. These two arms of social control, while ultimately proving completely ineffective against the forces of subversion, were able to completely suppress the forces that attempted to form to resist subversion, and thus allowed America to be destroyed during the Civil Rights Error.

The COINTELPRO program (which was, in part, investigated by the father of the writer, as a staffer on the Joint Congressional Committee on Intelligence Activities and the Rights of Americans), was the effort of the FBI, in coordination with other intelligence and law enforcement agencies, to suppress American political dissent that "threatened democracy." In that mission statement the fundamental error was contained, as democracy was itself but a stage in the decay of human society, and thus could never have formed a true center for resistance against the forces of the Dark Age. Thus, American law enforcement and intelligence found itself waging a war against both the forces of greater subversion and those who represented a true Traditional center of resistance to those forces—and thus their effort promoted and assisted the forces that they believed they would oppose.

The key goal of the American security forces was to prevent opposition to American democracy from being able to organize, and their tactics in this struggle were to not only disrupt, subvert and divide such opposition, but to decapitate it and target the leaders of such opposition, so as to render them politically ineffective. The arrest of American citizens who are identified as leaders in political movements believed opposed to democratic ideologies became a key aspect of the latter portion of this effort, while the spread of false propaganda about such leaders and organizations was a key aspect of the former. In this effort, the Jewish owned and Jewish controlled mass media gladly assisted—when the targets were the opponents of the forces of world subversion that such mass media represented. This assistance from the rest of the American establishment was key in the success of the security forces mission to destroy centers of Traditional resistance to anti-Traditional movements.

By the late 1960s, the destruction of the culture that had defined America prior to the Civil Rights Error was certain, and violent resistance to such destruction, as well as violent efforts to further such destruction, had become commonplace. Essentially every American president from Kennedy through Reagan was the subject of assassination attempts, and anti-Zionist or anti-communist forces were involved in essentially every attempt except the successful assassination of Kennedy—which gives every appearance of having been an operation conducted by the Jewish Mossad through the medium of the Jewish-Italian organized crime alliances of the mid-20th century. On the other side of the coin, Jewish-backed agitators, in the Negro community and without, were leading street level violence and riotous uprisings against the American government in many if not most American cities. It is in this context that the efforts of the American security forces must be understood.

The "neo-Nazi" movement, bizarrely named by Jewish intellectuals who need to append suffixes and prefixes to understand the political world, which to them is a wholly man made and essentially material invention, became, during the 1950s and 1960s, a breeding ground for the socially dysfunctional, and thus was able to produce a string of killers, assassins and serial killers that ultimately led to its discrediting and inability to break into the mainstream of public consciousness. A key factor in this was the holocaust lie, which, combined with maudlin Jewish accounts of wartime atrocities, linked National Socialism in the public consciousness with torture and death, and thus caused individuals with an interest in torture and death to gravitate toward it. Often combined with sexual dysfunction, these decadent elements became the defining element of "extremist" resistance to the power structure, and they were, ultimately, used by the Jews and the American security forces to discredit the movement to preserve white society and culture against communist and Jewish corruption.

That the movement against racism was also a movement in favor of murder, rape, pedophilia, cruelty and torture was obscured by a mass media intent upon focusing upon the nominally lofty "ideals" that communism represented. But the role of "white supremacists" in acts of seemingly random violence were given wide exposure until they completely eclipsed the truly lofty goals that define white resistance to world subversion. Thus, the fact that the communist Negro Martin Luther King, Jr.—still upheld as a model of Negro-communist virtue—regularly engaged in sadomasochistic abuse of prostitutes, white and black, often while shouting racial slurs and making comments like "I ain't a Negro tonight," is virtually unknown, where the fact that the "leaders" of many "white supremacist" groups are homosexuals and pedophiles is widely alleged.

Thus the American Nazi Party and its splinters produced James Earl Ray, John Hinckley, Jr. and Joseph Paul Franklin, among many, many others—and this became a trend embraced by other nominally "National Socialist" leaders—a trend that culminated in the embrace by National Socialism of Charles Manson and of the Church of Satan, two unique products of the cultural breakdown of the Civil Rights Error that would not normally have found any intersection with Traditional resistance to American society.

Charles Manson was the leader of a small hippie commune in the California desert, where he preached a doctrine of racial war that he believed would lead to the extermination of American whites—who lacked the will to resist a takeover of their society by Negro and communist forces—and the emergence of a black-dominated society that would need, after its ascension, white advisors who would be revered as gods—as the whites who had brought culture to all of the dark peoples of the world had been originally revered as gods. Thus, he preached that men and women should drop out of society and take to the wilderness, waiting for the collapse of America, so that they could emerge and take the world over; this was the *raison d'être* for his commune.

In the late 1960s, his followers conducted a series of murders which culminated in the murder of Sharon Tate, a sexually exploited white actress, her unborn child, and a number of Jews with whom she had been involved in pedophilia, sado-masochistic sex and the abuse and rape of children. Tate and the circle around her had been selling drugs to the Manson family, and they ripped Manson off. Manson was convicted of ordering their deaths, though he never participated in the killings, and the deaths were made to look as if they had been conducted by black revolutionaries—part of an effort to exacerbate racial tensions in the United States.

While really a case of cult versus cult, the murders fixated the attention of the United States on Manson's doctrines, which were, perhaps, too close to the doctrines that the forces of Jewish world subversion were already putting into practice. Manson and his actions also focused the attention of a number of members of American Nazi Party sympathizers, who elevated his acts to that of a political revolutionary, and which embraced him—and the effort of his disciple, Lynette "Squeaky" Fromm, to assassinate President Ford in retaliation for Manson's conviction.

Similar in genre to the embrace of Charles Manson was the embrace of the Church of Satan by activists who emerged from the American Nazi Party and its successors. The Church of Satan had been founded by the Jew Howard Stanton Levi, a carnival showman who changed his name in the 1960s to Anton LaVey and initiated a religion based upon the worship of sex and violence. Though typically Jewish in its reduction of humanity to a merely material and individualized being, the exaltation of destructive power—the Shiva element of the Aryan soul—attracted those who had been similarly attracted to neo-Nazism based upon its alleged association with destruction, cruelty, torture and death.

This association of National Socialism with death and murder did more to marginalize and subvert true resistance to the
forces of world destruction than any other factor. Other movements—the Southern rights movement, which has gone under
a variety of names as it has lost ground and shifted its goals
from defense of segregation to defense of the Confederate flag;
the "conservative" movement; various movements to preserve
the American Constitution—all failed because they placed their
center upon an earlier form of world subversion. The National
Socialist resistance to the Civil Rights Error failed because it embraced the destruction and death, cruelty and torture, which
defined its enemies and which its enemies inverted and use to
define it.

CHAPTER SEVEN

THE NEW WORLD ORDER

Following the ascension to power of a Jewish-communist elite during the social disorder of the Civil Rights Error came the concentration of power in the hands of a changed conservative elite and the establishment of the New World Order—the new system of control that replaced the dichotomy of Soviet communism and London-based capitalism that had defined the 19th and most of the 20th centuries. This New World Order began with the administration of Richard Nixon and the withdrawal of the United States from the international gold standard, and has culminated in the ascension to power of the Marxist mulatto Barack Obama as president of the United States. With it has come the rise and the beginning of the fall of the United States as the sole world governing body, and the foundations of the coming final step in the destruction of humankind, which is the establishment of a one world slave state that reduces all men under it to the same lowest level, burning up human life and bringing it to a terrible, tortuous end after an existence of degradation and misery. This future—the unlimited obliteration of the human race—is what the Jews and the Negroes have chosen for mankind, and is the fate that was foretold millennia past by the gods who first gave Aryan man human culture and society.

In the postwar period, the international banks reestablished their control under American dominion with the Bretton Woods Agreement—the agreement that created the World Bank, International Money Fund, and the system of international exchange continues to define the modern banking system. This system was the system that transitioned the decolonized nations into dependence upon the old British-based banking system, with the exception that the old London-based system had been largely moved by its Jewish paymasters to New York.

From the Bretton Woods agreement come the roots of the modern system of international capitalism that cold-warred against and eventually supplanted the Soviet Union, neutralizing the threat of international communism by replacing it with the threat of international democracy. The principles that were established at Bretton Woods—those of international trade and international capital traversing a world without borders—constitute the economic side of the restructuring of global power known as the New World Order—the order that culminates in the rise of the slave states that are doomed to destroy human life on this planet. While the Bretton Woods system nominally placed the United States in the position once held by the British empire, its real effect was to dismantle all national boundaries, as those same national boundaries had once sought to dismantle all ethnic differentiation within the national borders.

Nixon took the first step in dismantling the economy of the United States when he took the American economy off of the international gold standard, by ordering that international American debts would no longer be payable from America's gold reserves. Though Franklin Roosevelt had stopped the use of gold for the payment of domestic debts in 1933, he had continued the use of gold in international transactions. While Nixon's acts were, in a sense, the perfection of American economic hegemony, in that Nixon declared that the fiat dollars issued by the Federal Reserve would now suffice for the payment of all American transactions, his acts were also the beginning of American economic collapse, as they completed the process of divorcing the measurement of the success of the American economy from anything real, and thus allowed the fantasies of the Jews directing the Federal Reserve to take control.

The first immediate effect of Nixon's actions was the massive inflation without economic growth that characterized the 1970s—so-called stagflation. Without any real limit on the ability of America to issue debt, America was able to print its money—linked to its debt—without limit, and hyper-inflate its economy. Yet there was no move by Nixon, Ford or Carter to increase the productive power of the American economy by encouraging the development of agriculture or industry. Instead, during this period the theory of free trade that would dominate American economic policy until the end of the 20th century was concocted by Jewish economists that sought to pursue the benefit of their people above and beyond the interests of the peoples residing within America.

During Nixon's administration one sees, for the first time since the end of World War II, a drop in wages in real terms among American workers—a drop that was largely disguised by an increase in wages in nominal terms that accompanied the expansion of the amount of currency in circulation. Thus an American who earned $8 an hour before Nixon would have been earning $10 an hour in actual currency afterward, but only been able to buy $6 worth of goods with it. America began to deindustrialize and de-agriculturalize—a two-prong policy that would define the domestic efforts of the Reagan, Bush and Clinton administrations.

With the collapse of real American wages came the expansion of credit for "ordinary" Americans—an expansion that was prompted by the lifting of the limitations on usurious rates of interest that had defined earlier American borrowing. Beginning in the 1970s, spurred in part by the invention of the credit card, and ending in the mid-1990s, international banks lobbied for and received not only changes at the state level in American usury laws, but obtained a number of Supreme Court decisions that allowed banks to charge interest without limit across state lines, as long as their corporate headquarters was located in a state that did not place a limit on usurious interest. Thus most international banks operating in the United States moved their headquarters to Delaware or North Dakota or a state that lacked interest laws, and then began to operate across state lines in states that did have usury laws, thus negating those laws and gaining the ability to exploit unsophisticated and often unqualified borrowers.

Thus the American economy transitioned into a two-tier currency—one the official "cash" printed by the Federal Reserve, and the other the ability of the individual to borrow on "credit" against their future earnings. Federal Reserve notes already represented a borrowing by the national government against its future tax revenues—a form of the mortgaging of the labor of working people—and the expansion of credit cards allowed individuals to mortgage the remainder of their earning power infinitely into the future. That this system collapsed within thirty (arguably forty, as there was a transition period) years should be no surprise, as such systems have always collapsed—but that collapse has provided the crisis that will likely end the New World Order period and give the Jewish-Masonic elite the excuse necessary to establish direct world totalitarian rule.

The 1970s are also noteworthy for the development of Judeo-Christianity, a movement claiming nominal resistance to the culture decline initiated by the world destroyers during the Civil Rights Error, but in reality another guise under which those powers of decline became manifest. A goal of the Jews since the earliest eras of their revolutions was to destroy and dismantle religion—thus the promotion and use of Protestant resistance to the Catholic Church during the first democratic revolutions of the 18th century. But with the effective dismantling of all Christian organizations during the mid-20th century, and the conversion of most Protestant Christian organizations to the theories and goals of world communism, seen as a perfection of the "original" Christian spirit of Jesus Christ, the return of Christianity was permitted by the Jews and Masons in a form that the world subverters could control. Realizing the need of different markets for different products, "right" and "left" wing versions of these anti-human doctrines were created, but their essential features—deification of the Jews, opposition to "racism," and support for social programs designed to perpetuate the existence of the worst elements of humanity, they held in common.

So the World Council of Churches could support the genocide and mass murder of innocent white people in Rhodesia under the name of communism, while Jerry Falwell could preach the divine necessity of the Zionist occupation of Palestine, and the Church of Christ could promote homosexuality, while all could come together and be part of the "Judeo-Christian" movement to promote "Christ" and his alleged doctrines within the modern world. That "Christianity" became compatible with the ritual human sacrifice of children, with the penetration of a man's anus by another man's penis, and the torture, rape and murder of white people by Jewish-supported Negroes, was seen as largely irrelevant, since Christ was planning to destroy this world and its evils anyway, and salvation was both solely individual and confined solely to the next world. What was key was that all of these anti-human "Christian" doctrines opposed the nominal "atheism" of Communism—and thus could claim opposition to the forces of world subversion.

Really, what the early stages of the New World Order heralded in was the complete divorce of American politics from any basis in reality. American politics had never been very good, and had always largely reflected the efforts of various criminal groups and bands of thieves to best use the government to plunder the American worker, but at times the ideological crises of American politics had been real. After World War II, all real dispute within the American political establishment vanished, and the only question became by what path the Jewish-Masonic elite could best and most efficiently loot the country while degrading and then murdering the entirety of its people. The neo-conservative Jews created a parody of what they believed "right-wing nationalism" had been, and placed it in the service of international communist revolution, while the older school of left-wing Jews subverted and bought the Democratic Party and the so-called "liberal" left. Both wings of Jewry then converged on the issues of internationalism and the destruction of the white race, and propagated these policies under various names in the way that a major corporation might sell different flavors of soda, knowing that all flavors are so loaded with sugar, caffeine and acid that their long-term effect is to poison the consumer. Thus, to one set of idiots the Jews sold internationalism, degradation and suicide under the name of "Judeo-Christianity," while to another set of idiots the same policies were sold under the name of "communism," and to a third they were sold under the name of "anti-communism" or "libertarianism."

The fact is that all Jewish ideologies and ways of being are essentially the same; they are all essentially evil; and none of them can form the basis for any set of personal morality. The only differences between the "right" and "left" in the post-Civil-Rights-Error United States is that of the differences between two football teams—they are two sets of people striving for the same goal, using the same tactics, under different names and symbols.

And it should be no surprise that the major American sporting leagues are dominated, in their ownership and management, by Jews in the same way as American politics—a formula that works so well in one area cannot be abandoned in another.

The Reagan administration marked the ascension to power of the neo-conservative Jews, and this is the main reason that Ronald Reagan continues to be deified by the conservative movement. Reagan did not substantially alter the direction of the United States—he merely perfected the navigation of the country along a path of collapse when that collapse had accelerated beyond the ability of the Jews to control it. If anything, the main effect of the Reagan Revolution was to consolidate Jewish control in such a way that the destruction of the United States became inevitable, while buying the Jews enough time to make sure that, in their looting of the country, they did not forget a thing.

Nixon had first normalized relations with Communist China, but it was Reagan that first granted China Most Favored Nation trading status. Reagan, too, had been a proponent of international trade, encouraging the transfer of the U.S. economy to Japan—a move that was only stalled by the collapse of the Japanese economy into stagnation during the later part of the 1980s and early 1990s. Reagan normalized the status of illegal Mexican immigrants within the United States, part of his larger plan to open the borders of the United States with Mexico and Central America, and also normalized the tens of thousands of Cuban emigres that had been ejected from Cuban prisons and mental hospitals onto the Florida coast. But most notable among Reagan's "achievements" was his centralization of control of American farmland in the hand of a few Jewish-owned food companies—a feat Reagan achieved by allowing interest rates to float to unimaginable highs, then allowing banks to foreclose and sell the farmland to Jewish land speculators, much in the manner of his ideological predecessors in the Weimar Republic. Since the Reagan administration, the small farmer has ceased to exist as an element of importance in the American political body.

In the reign of Reagan's successor, his Vice President George Bush, the Soviet Union collapsed, its armed forces unable to afford to cope with a worldwide struggle against CIA-financed narco-terrorism. The Soviet Union had chosen to engage the United States in a world theater, instead of truly struggling for the benefit of the peoples that it governed over, and its initial successes had come from the fact that the United States had little to offer the colored peoples of the world except a "freedom" that came inextricably linked with poverty. But the creation of drug-distribution networks as cartels and organized crime gave America an alternative to offer the world's poor—they could have the sluggardly industrialization and economic development that came with Soviet communism, or they could have the fast money and power that came from selling drugs with American support. In the minds of the characteristically lazy non-white peoples of the world, drug money beat working any day, and thus the United States was able to attack the Soviet Union all over the world through drug-financed terrorist proxies and so drain the Soviet military that the USSR could not both support its occupations and client states and support itself. As the Soviet Union always represented an essential occupation of the lands it governed by a Jewish minority, and did so very explicitly, when it became unable to afford its soldiers, its people cast it aside—and embraced, ironically, Jewish capitalist robber barons and "democratic" states largely of their making—all in accordance with the American model.

Of course these policies of the conservatives of the Reagan administration carried "blowback," and the major non-state actors challenging the current effort to consolidate global rule are the narco-terrorist networks, whether Latin or Islamic, that the United States put in place to control and contain the Soviet Union. Further, the effect of these narco-terrorist networks and the expansion of drug distribution within the United States utilizing paths that the CIA and the conservatives carved for them was devastating to white working people, who found that, through the abuse of drugs, they became enslaved to the predatory Negro underclass that the conservatives had chosen to distribute their drugs. While crack cocaine may have been aimed at the black community through black gangs, the practical effect of the CIA's organization of black and Latin drug gangs in the United States was to subject white working people to not only exploitation by Negro drug dealers, but to a massive rise in the pimping and prostitution of white working women by drug-involved Negro pimps. In some American cities, it is commonplace to see crack or heroin junkies—white and female—who became addicted in their youth after exposure to Negro culture being sold on the street for perhaps $10 or a cigarette per sex act in a desperate effort to keep themselves and some homeless Negro junkie who is pimping them alive. This degradation of the most vulnerable elements of the white race—that 15% of white people who are no brighter than Negroes and no better able to behave—is the direct result of the election of Ronald Reagan and George Bush and the unfettered efforts of their intelligence cronies in the Federal Bureau of Investigation and the Central Intelligence Agency.

So while the Reagan administration was responsible for encouraging the overreach of the Jew-communist empire of the Soviet Union, and thus bankrupted it, it also created the enemies that it would then contest in its own nation's efforts to forge a democratic empire in the decades that followed.

Domestically, Reagan also set the foundation for the economic crisis that came to embrace the United States in the 21st century. Rather than correcting the error of the Nixon administration in releasing all restraints on American spending by allowing American currency to float internationally, rather than be tied to gold or, on the German model, American production, Reagan was a dupe of the capitalist-libertarian school of Jewish finance—the school founded by the failed central banker Ludwig von Mises—and opened America's borders as widely as possible to the middle-manning of American goods and labor by the Jews. Reagan particularly wished to use Japan for these purposes, and the Japanization of American culture and economy was a major news story during the 1980s—a news story that was cut short by the failure and stagnation of the Japanese economy. After several successors were attempted, it would be during the late part of the first Bush administration and the Clinton administration that a growing economy capable of producing the cheap goods necessary to destroy the American economy would be found in China—with its service equivalent, the growing economy of India.

Reagan also opened the borders of the United States to illegal immigration, "normalizing" the status of over two million illegal immigrants already in the United States, and allowing their relatives to enter the country and further disembowel and hollow out American productive industry and agriculture. The Latino population, white and non-white, of the United States began its explosion under Reagan, not only through immigration, but through the encouragement of the resettlement of communist guerrillas—the remnants of the MS-13 resistance in El Salvador, in American cities—the foundation of much of the modern American gang problem.

Lastly, there are Reagan's infamous inflation policies, which made the debts of many small Americans who had mortgaged their land during the inflation of the 1970s unpayable, and allowed the major Jewish agricultural concerns to consolidate their control of American farmland—a process which led directly to the 1990s reaction known as the militia movement, and the campaign against "domestic terror" which has so occupied the American mindset since the government staged the Oklahoma City bombing in 1995. Reagan appointed to the Federal Reserve Alan Greenspan, a disciple of Ludwig von Mises, and the reaction against Greenspan's exploitation and theft of the land and labor of the American worker can be compared to the reaction his predecessor found in Austria, when mobs of Austrian workers and peasants lynched his boss and chased him out of the country—never to return. Unfortunately, the American resistance to this latest round of Jewish exploitation was less successful.

Reagan's policies were followed by his successor, George Bush, who initiated the conflict in the Middle East that would explode ten years later into the War on Terrorism. Saddam Hussein had been a petty anti-communist dictator that had crushed the Soviet-funded Kurdish resistance in Iraq, as well as the Iranian-financed Shi'ite Muslim resistance in the south, and thus had been encouraged by the United States as a counterweight against its enemies and the enemies of its Zionist masters in Palestine. Yet, by the early 1990s, Hussein had become inconvenient, as his pan-Arab nationalist ideology had turned against the Zionists in Palestine and had led to his financing of suicide bombings that were effectively destabilizing the Jewish effort to control Palestinian lands. The weight of the issue turned against him, and Bush decided to limit him—while retaining him as a counterweight, this time against Iranian and Syrian expansion in the region.

The Zionists had founded their entity in 1948 with the genocide of the people of Palestine. Having killed everyone they could locate, they then declared, with typical chutzpah, that the land had been "found empty" and that they could therefore assert their "birthright" and occupy it. However, the Jews that seized Palestine were not the Hebrews of the Old Testament— they were, primarily, the Khazars of the Ukrainian plain that had been crushed in the 10th century by Sviatoslav of Kiev, and who had since infiltrated and poisoned the Nordic-Germanic culture that once destroyed them, rising to such a position of prominence that they were able to claim an entire state as a base for their international criminal operations.

Originally, the Zionists had found support in the Soviet Union, a fellow Jewish monstrosity, but this support quickly eroded as the formless internationalism of the "ex-"Trotskyites of the West became the guiding ideology of the Zionist occupa- tion—and thus found itself inexorably in conflict with Soviet imperialism. Stalin, having expelled from the Kremlin most of the Jews he had found there, had become unpopular with all but the hardest-core of the old-line Jewish communists, and the foundation of the Zionist Occupation became the corner- stone of the next tactic—which was to have a base of operations for the historically successful tactic of infiltration and manipu- lation of gentile cultures.

Thus the Soviets aligned themselves against the Zionist oc- cupation, providing material and support to the Arab nation- alists who opposed it, and the anti-communist wing of the United States was further persuaded to align itself with Jewish interests, promoting Jews to positions of influence and absorb- ing into its ideology the ideology of international Jewry—an ideology which paralleled the communist ideology that the anti-communists thought they were opposing.

Under Reagan this infiltration and control of the "right"- wing "opposition" to the openly communist American "left" wing was complete, and the "neo"-conservatives were thus able to wage a political war against the "paleo"-conservatives which nominally opposed them, driving gentiles from positions of power in the Republican Party under the guide of "fighting racism" and "anti-Semitism," and consolidating complete control over all the institutions of the American political system.

The first George Bush was perhaps the last president to maintain even nominal independence from the control of the Jews, and even he was compelled to hand his military operations over to a mulatto "general" and make "diversity" the public face of his administration. Bush's refusal to follow the Jews all the way and destroy Saddam Hussein—a disastrous policy whose implications we are only beginning to see in the current decade—cost him his presidency, as all of the organs of Jewish media control turned against him and declared him a "wimp," a phony appeal to the pseudo-machismo promoted in the Jew media so-called "conservatives" and "American patriots" have bought into. Yet his refusal to destroy Hussein—an unnecessary move that promoted no American interest—was probably one of the most sensible decisions of his presidency.

In the 1990s, the Republican Party met its greatest challenge with the presidential campaign of Ross Perot, which would have been successful had the candidate himself not been such a flake. Pat Buchanan, within the Republican Party, had led an anti-internationalist wing whose opposition to Jewish "democracy" infuriated the Jews while creating no effective traditional center of resistance—particularly as Buchanan himself could not break the constraints of democratic-Constitutionalism and the phony pseudo-traditional "centers" created by the lesser decadence of the American revolution. But outside the Republican Party, Perot ran explicitly on a platform of anti-internationalism, opposition to the free trade policies of the Bush and Reagan administrations, and for the rebuilding of the American economy on an independent basis. His platform was wildly popular, but he was unable to take the pressures of the internationalists who opposed him, and withdrew from the race claiming he was in danger of assassination from black helicopters that were following him. He may have been correct in this assertion—but no man lives forever, and Perot had lived just long enough to see the disastrous destruction of the country he refused to stand up and save.

Perot's introduction into the presidential race allowed Bill Clinton to win the presidency with a minority, and Clinton took up the policies of Reagan and Bush with renewed vigor, imposing on the United States the North American Free Trade Agreement and further opening American borders—particularly to China, which was identified by the Jews, early in the Clinton presidency, as the best alternative to the failed economy of Japan. Clinton's China policies allowed the creation of Wal-Mart, and his domestic economic policies allowed the expansion of usury and the international banks by legalizing "fees" and "payday lendings"—two practices which further bled the pockets of the poor who had, in ignorance, turned out in droves for Clinton and his Jewish paymasters.

Clinton's administration also marked the beginning of the phony war on terror, which was initiated by the federal government's bombing of the Oklahoma City building under the guise of militia opponents, who had been recruited and pushed into the act by the Federal Bureau of Investigation, part of an operation that eventually drew in the current attorney general, Eric Holder. Though it has taken over a decade for the documents to be revealed—and those have only come out through a massive court battle fought in Salt Lake City by the brother of the federal informant who was tortured and murdered in return for his cooperation—the federal government, working with a Jewish homosexual group called the Southern Poverty Law Center, had infiltrated the "militia movement," particularly a radical religious compound called Elohim City, and identified a number of unstable individuals they thought they could use to create a major terrorist act on American soil. The Federal Bureau of Investigation recruited an informant, Andreas Strassmeier, who had already been working for the Southern Poverty Law Center, and another man, Roger Moore, a local gun dealer. Working through Moore, the FBI provided explosives to Timothy McVeigh and Terry Nichols—leaving behind the fingerprints of two agents on the explosives' casings. Not all of the Kinestick detonators provided by the FBI were used by the two, and, at some point during the operation, the federal government lost track and control of McVeigh and Nichols—who used a portion of the Kinestick detonators Moore provided to destroy the Oklahoma City federal building, as Clinton and elements within the FBI had planned. The FBI rushed to find the remaining explosives—but couldn't. The FBI missed them during a search of the Nichols's home. Ten years later, Nichols would finally reveal the location—and the FBI would race to recover the explosives just ahead of Homeland Security.

The FBI was able to arrest McVeigh and Nichols so quickly because they already knew who they were—co-conspirators with the FBI itself. The FBI also arrested a third man in the conspiracy—Richard Lee Guthrie. An innocent man, Kenneth Michael Trentadue, was mistaken for Guthrie at the Oklahoma City Transfer Center, and subsequently tortured to death by the guards—an act for which the Bureau of Prisons eventually paid $1.1 million dollars to Trentadue's family. This money has financed a major lawsuit by Jesse Trentadue, Kenneth Trentadue's brother, that led to the uncovering of documentation of the extensive role the FBI played in creating the OKC attack. A series of corrupt actions, including the murder of two other prisoners believed to have evidence about the Oklahoma City case, possibly ordered by Eric Holder, have surrounded the Trentadue investigation.

The Jews wanted to stage a major terrorist act on American

soil for several reasons. One was the massive failure of their gun control efforts, which they viewed as a necessary prerequisite for totalitarian control in the United States—much as it had been a prerequisite for similar control in other Western nations. The fact that the gun lobby in the United States was largely controlled by the same Jewish interests that the Jews who opposed private gun ownership represented was irrelevant—there had always been dissent within the Jwish monolith. So, while the NRA, founded as a collection of Union Army officers, had promoted the Jewish line that guns were only for "sports" and "hunting," and not for armed resistance against tyranny, the Jews remained dissatisfied and worked for the final destruction of the already eroded gun rights of the American people. However, legislation introduced in 1995 to achieve this as part of a measure to control "domestic terrorism" failed—and thus a bombing was needed to kick-start the "war on terror."

However, the campaign against terrorism by white Americans still clinging to the lie of American constitutionalism and the American "democratic" revolution did not proceed as well as the Jews had planned, and led to a new campaign of pseudo-resistance that resulted in the election of a "right-wing" president that was able to wage a "war on terror" much more efficiently than that which the Jews of the left-wing had conceived. Knowing that, while American remained a country with a white majority, that majority could be divided, but never united, against itself, the Jews of the right wing realized that, in order to initiate a "war on terrorism," they needed an external enemy—and thus the enemies of the Jewish occupation of Palestine—the Muslim and Arab nations—were chosen.

The "war on terror" was first fought by Joseph Stalin, and the same rhetoric which today characterizes the American crusade for domestic tyranny was invented by the Soviet regime in the mid-1930s, when the assassination of a mayor of

Leningrad—and major rival of Stalin—by an alleged opponent of the regime gave Stalin the excuse he needed to begin the massive purges that characterized the genocide of 1937 and 1938. While this purge largely eliminated the Jewish-Trotskyite faction of the communist hierarchy, their heirs would later use it as their model for the elimination of their domestic "conservative" political opposition.

Just as the Jewish left had attempted to start a war on white Americans by staging the bombing of the Oklahoma City Federal Building, the Jewish right decided to start a war that would target both Islam and white America by launching the attack that destroyed the World Trade Center towers in New York City. With the assistance of the Zionist government in Palestine, the Jews were able to recruit out of the CIA-founded al Qaeda operation 20 men who hijacked airliners and drove them into both of the World Trade Center towers and the American Pentagon in Washington, D.C.—with a fourth plane, destined for the Capitol or the White House, failing to reach its target. That the Zionists knew of the attack has been clear since it was released that a Zionist instant messaging company sent notices to all of its employees at the World Trade Center not to report to work, and since the roundup of over 200 Zionist spies in the United States after the bombing revealed a network that had not only scouted the targets, but had videotaped the attacks and danced and celebrated as the trade towers came down. Further, it is clear that the Zionist in the United States were prepared for the attack, as they were able, before any information had come in, to not only identify the origin of the attack, but to launch a massive propaganda campaign designed to further their interests, both in the evisceration of America, and in the destruction of their Arab enemies.

Thus, early in the administration of the second Bush, the Zionists were able to perfect the plan for total control and final destruction of the United States that they had first attempted under the Clinton administration. The response of the Bush administration was knee-jerk and as predictable as Bush's adherence to the lies of the Judaized-Christian religion. The Zionists handed Bush a plan for the occupation and destruction of the entire Islamic world, from Pakistan to Libya, and Bush marched along with it.

The attacks on Iraq and Afghanistan have to be viewed in the context of the Jewish effort to gain total control over southern Asia and the Middle East. While, in the middle of the 20th century, Arab nationalist movements had been useful to the Jews in their efforts to destroy the rotting remnants of the colonial empires of the Western powers, and the late part of the 20th century, Islamic resistance movements had been a useful counterweight against the anti-Zionist Soviet Union, both, in the 20th century, represented manifestations of a Traditional culture that was healthier, more independent, and more dangerous than the rotten and subverted culture of Judaized America. Having gained nearly total control of the Western nations, and having, during the 1990s, gained control of much of post-Soviet east Europe in a series of coups and bribes, the Jews were ready to turn against the previously underdeveloped portions of the world that had resisted them—the strongest basin of which were the Islamic nations of southern Asia, and, in particular, Iran.

While the Arab nations had been responsible for the constant armed resistance to the Jewish occupation of Palestine, Iran had proven itself, during the Persian-Arab conflict of the 1980s, to be vastly strongly and superior to those nations, as the Zionist Entity, with American military support, had proven itself in the 1970s. Its intelligence service was well developed and it had regional influence over significant factions of all of its neighbors—as well as a religious alliance based on Shi'ite Islam with the minority Alawite government of Syria. The resistance movements it financed in the region were superior to the resistance movements that had been financed by independent Arab nations, and it posed the strongest center of resistance to the global Zionist agenda.

Thus, while the Jews certainly hated the government of Saddam Hussein, and had been in conflict with the American intelligence community on the issue of his retention of deposition, they also needed to target nations such as Afghanistan, which posed little threat themselves to Jewish control of the region, but were a necessary part of the campaign to encircle and eventually destroy Iran. That the Taliban government in Afghanistan had harbored the leaders of the organization that had conducted the attacks was well known to the Zionists when they organized the 9-11 campaign, and that the Taliban practiced a radical version of Islam that would help define in the American mind the foreign enemy needed to justify domestic repression was well known as well. In fact, much about Al Qaeda was well known to the Jews, as they had worked with the American CIA in creating it during the 1980s.

So the war drive of the 21st century began, and the American government bankrupted itself attacking and occupying the nations of Iraq and Afghanistan, as the first move in a campaign against Iran which America was never able to afford, and could never even begin, as the difficulties in occupying two foreign nations in which American had no interest prevented the establishment of a stable base for further action. During the Bush administration, these two failed war effort were the major factor in the bankrupting of the American government; during Obama, other spending concerns quickly eclipsed it, as America hurtled over the edge into complete financial collapse.

Domestically, Bush was as much a terrorist as the Jews wished him to be. With the demand to wage war on the last Traditional culture remaining on the Earth, came the demand to begin domestic repression in the Soviet style—the demand to arrest domestic enemies and to torture them; to increase government monitoring of private citizens; to increase security measures and to limit travel domestically; and to regulate the private use of currency through increased monitoring and reporting. While few of these measures have ever proven effective in fighting "terrorism," they did allow for the increased ability of the government to manufacture the phony terrorist plots that are the bread and butter of their so-called war.

During Stalin's "war on terror," the Soviet government would often discover "plots" that were complete fabrications, but whose reality was broadcast in the media and accepted by the courts, and which were used to manipulate and terrorize the people over whom the communists governed. In the United States, the government now engages in the same policy, creating terrorist plots that never existed and widely publicizing the arrest of the victims and stooges in them in order to create the illusion that the country is constantly under siege.

The roots of this law enforcement effort lie in the Reagan administration, when laws, allegedly to fight "organized crime" were introduced with the "war on drugs" that not only generally denied bail to all federal inmates, but eliminated most of the constitutional rights in the federal system and vastly expanded the use of "inchoate crime" laws, such as conspiracy and solicitation, to arrest and prosecute individuals for crimes that had never occurred and were either impossible or unlikely to occur. Thus, two men talking about selling drugs that didn't exist and which they could never obtain could be arrested for a "drug conspiracy" and held in prison for thirty years or more—and, similarly, two Americans discussing armed resistance to the American government could be arrested and charged with "seditious" or "terrorist" conspiracy and held in prison for an even longer period—though they never intended to engage in any armed uprising or act of terrorism, and never had the ability to do so.

The 1990s saw the beginning of the use of these laws in combating "domestic terrorists," were FBI informants would join—or sometimes create—militia groups, then use those groups to promote violence, suggest to the members that they engage in terrorism, and then arrest everyone involved for "conspiracy" to commit an act that was not only impossible, but in which even the intent was, at best, cryptic and dubious. Knowing that the American people had been terrorized into fighting terrorism at every level, such cases stood little chance before a jury. With all constitutional safeguards having been eliminated during the "war on drugs," such men, if they declared the government's efforts a lie, faced sentences as much as a third longer, and thus were often forced to plea, in the hopes that they would survive to be released in their old age. Thus the government, by compelling such pleas, was able to maintain the illusion of truth behind their web of lies.

With the normalization of torture in the 21st century, government arrests of American political dissidents for nominal or non-existent crimes expanded, and the government became bolder, knowing that few men could resist confessing falsely under torture, and that the Bond Reform Act of 1986 would guarantee that any man accused of a crime could be detained— usually for months—and tortured pending trial—thus guaranteeing his false confession. Upon this basis, the Obama administration would attempt to initiate a new round of arrests for domestic terrorism, alleging a "neo-Nazi" and "white supremacist" terror conspiracy.

The "war on terror" also provided Bush with cover for the final destruction of the American economy, as credit finally expanded, under his reign, to the point where the American economy collapse, much as it had during the Weimar Republic in the 1930s. With few jobs left, the elimination of the usury laws, which was completed under the Clinton government, allowed the banks to loan money on real estate and credit cards to provide Americans with the purchasing power they could no longer find through productive employment. Thus real assets and American labor were mortgaged to the fullest—and beyond the fullest—to levels that their actual value could not support. This caused, during the middle of the first decade of the 21st century a massive inflation in the value of real and capital assets that collapse when the ability of the system to provide credit to by them became so overstretched that it could not provide money even in its imagination. The American dollar by this time had nothing real behind it, and was a wholly imaginary unit—but even the imagination of the Jewish bankers had its limits, and, near the end of the second Bush term, they could not even imagine handing out more money to the bankrupted American workers they had exploited.

Thus, near the end of the Bush administration, the American economy collapsed, and many American banks, including several prominent ones, failed, along with several large American businesses. As a stopgap measure, the Bush administration ordered the Jewish bankers of the Federal Reserve to provide more capital—and those bankers, in terror of the collapse of a system before they were prepared for it, agreed. Thus American debt, which was already spiraling out of control, and which had been linked to the issuance of American currency since the decision of the Nixon administration to float the currency on the international markets, was expanded to the point where it became clear to everyone—even the collaborators of the New World Order in other nations—that an eventual American default was inevitable.

The failure of the American economy, combined with the failure of American war policy, led to the election of the current black communist government whose reign in the United States has been so controversial—and has been accompanied with a new round of domestic resistance that has, so far, been controlled by the nominal Jewish-led opposition among the Republicans.

While the Obama government has made no major breaks from the policies the American government has pursued since Reagan, except, perhaps, that it further attempted to expand the welfare policies of the government through the introduction of a national health care system—a system whose brief existence did little but further bankrupt the already bankrupt economy— its explicitly Marxist orientation and its failure to address the problems created by the previous administrations have made it an easy target for the phony-Americanism of the Jewish right.

Obama himself can almost hardly be blamed for the troubles his government has faced, or his own unpopularity, as he came up in politics as a creature of the rich Jewish elite in Chicago, and has been largely subservient to them throughout his career. He was selected by them as a figurehead, and as a man easily manipulated and controlled by them, not least of all because of his inexperience, and he has had little independent input into his own government. While Bush and, to a lesser degree, Clinton, represented independent elements of the American governing establishment, Obama was a pure pawn of the men and women who created him—and thus he could hardly do anything except what he was told: to continue the decadence and destruction that have characterized these final decades of the United States.

The failure of the United States, its wars, its economy, and its occupations have led to numerous consequences in the international sphere—consequences Obama and his backers have tried to contain and control, but which are clearly ultimately uncontrollable, not least of all due to the financial and military weakness of the American government. The most notable has been the so-called "Arab spring," which has overturned several American and former Soviet client states in the Middle East, not out of demand for greater liberality, but out of demand for greater adherence to the principles of Islam. While America has controlled this in Egypt by buying a new government with its billions in foreign aid, and controlled this in Libya by allowing its socialist partners in NATO to support the al Qaeda rebellion against the government of Muammar Qadaffi, it has been unable to utilize these rebellions to overthrow Arab nationalist or Islamic states such as those of Syria and Iran. Further, these rebellions have allowed the government American established in Iraq to further ally itself with the Shi'ite Iranian-Syrian bloc, a move that will likely lead to the diminishment and eventual expulsion of American influence and forces from Mesopotamia.

The United States has seriously destabilized and caused an armed rebellion in Pakistan that has to be seen as a serious challenge to the Pakistani government—a government that was firmly allied with the Islamic government of Afghanistan before the American invasion. Pakistan, which has always seen its greatest threat in the socialist and Hindu nation of India, and which has historically rooted itself in its Islamic culture, is now faced with an Islamic resistance that undercuts the logic of its government's existence, and has created a crisis that its government can only maintain, for the moment, with naked force. Pakistan is, of course, one of the world's nuclear nations, and its collapse into the emerging Shi'ite Islamic sphere would be disastrous for the very Zionists who created the movements that are destabilizing it.

In the world of international finance, the collapse of the American dollar has led the powers of Eurasia to seek alternatives to U.S. hegemony, and it is likely the second decade of the 21st century will see Russia, China and India break from Bretton Woods and create a new system of international exchange—one that will likely be independent of the Jewish-Western banks, if Russia's purge of its Jewish billionaires and financiers is any indication of its intentions in the international arena. Of course, Russia has become a target of American Jewry and its puppets in the Senate, particularly John McCain, who were not amused at the destruction of the Zionist client state that had been established in Georgia during the brief 2008 Russian-Georgian war. But, despite the successful efforts of George Soros and his fellow Jewish billionaires to launch coups in Georgia, Ukraine and several former members of the Soviet sphere in the 1990s, the reestablishment of Russian power has largely constrained their efforts in recent years, as the Russian government has worked to reestablish itself and challenge the fading power of the United States.

Domestically, the American economy is and has been in a state of collapse from which no recovery appears possible. Of course, the re-establishment of domestic industry and agriculture—the re-creation of the productive power of the American economy—would quickly solve the problem, but the wealth and power of the Jews is so dependent on internationalism that they are incapable of implementing such a solution, even to save themselves. Thus the doom of America—a democratic "empire" whose power in the 20th century was entirely dependent upon its wealth—has been sealed. The country is bankrupt and dedicated to the policies that created its bankruptcy, while the same Jewish financiers who have destroyed the country control its culture and media, and now have in their bag of tricks repressive laws that can be used to arrest, torture, railroad and murder any political opposition—a combination of factors that make any independent political resistance to the failed and bankrupt American regime impossible.

Sheep graze near the ruins of the German Frauenkirche in 1957. The church —and many thousands like it—was reduced to rubble during World War II Allied bombings. The debris remained for five decades. The church was finally restored and reconsecrated for the 60th anniversary of its destruction.

MEN AMONG THE RUINS

Having laid out the ascension to power of ancient demonic forces that are intent upon degrading and destroying the entirety of the human race, it is reasonable if the reader would ask what I believe can or should be done about it. But then, to ask that question is to ignore all that I and the Aryan prophecy I have quoted from have said can and should be done about it—the sum of which is, essentially, nothing. Time is the Great Destroyer and it is going to destroy the world; the Aryan can resist it, and, in that resistance, he can find eternal life in the next world. But this world is doomed to be destroyed, and the only thing that the Aryan can do in this final stage of the Kali Yuga is to hasten upon this world its own destruction—first, by exterminating the masses of lesser humankind that the Jews have produced to feed their evil gods; and, second, by seeking and finding death, filling the halls of Valhalla and hastening the coming of that time when the last Arya shall die and the earth, bereft of worthy mankind, shall be burned.

Those who view the current crisis as a political confrontation and a creation of mere human forces are those who are wont to seek a political solution or to make a political effort against the crisis. Democracy offers many apparent avenues by which change can be effected, and the foolish are inclined to follow them, not least of all because they seem "safe" and because participation in orderly society is the natural inclination of the white race. What such men cannot grasp is that the current social order is not legitimate, and thus any compliance with such an order is a contribution to the evil that is consuming the world, and makes those that participate in it as culpable in the world's destruction as the guiding forces behind the democratic system.

Every white activist should reflect upon the words of Max Stirner, in understanding the relationship of our movement against culture destruction to the state of the culture destroyers:

"The state allows me to realize value from all my thoughts and to find customers for them—but only so long as my thoughts are its thoughts. If, on the other hand, I harbor thoughts that it cannot approve, then it does not allow me to realize any value from them, to bring them into exchange, into commerce. My thoughts are free only if they are granted to me by the state's grace, if they are the state's thoughts. It lets me philosophize freely only so far as I approve myself a 'philosopher of the state'; against the state I must not philosophize, though gladly it tolerate me helping it out of its 'deficiencies', 'furthering' it.

"The state has nothing to be more afraid of than the value of me, and nothing must more carefully guard against than every occasion that offers itself to me for realizing value from myself. I am the deadly enemy of the state, which always hovers between the alternatives, it or I.

". . .People do not yet know what they mean when they cry for liberty . . . But they ostensibly ask is that the state shall set the[m] free; but they are really after, without knowing it themselves, is that the[y] become free from the state, or clear of the state. . . . A 'petition for right', even as a serious demanding of the right of liberty . . . presupposes the state as the giver, and can hope only for a present, a permission, a chartering. Possible, no doubt, that a state acts so senselessly as to grant the demanded present but you may bet everything that those who receive the present will not know how to use it so long as they regard the state as a truth; they will not trespass against this 'sacred thing,' and will call for a penal . . . law against everyone who would be willing to dare this.

"Do I here perhaps show myself an opponent of liberty . . . ? On the contrary, I only assert that one will never get it if one wants only it . . . if one sets only for an unrestricted permission. Only beg right along for this permission: you may wait forever for it, for there is no one in the world who could give it to you. As long as you want to have yourselves 'entitled' . . . by a permission, you live in vain . . .

"Let my people, if they will, go without liberty . . . I will manage it by force or ruse; I get my permission only from myself—and my strength. . . . I am not concerned for permission, but so much the more for their folly and their overthrow."

Stirner, though he attacked all things, knew that he was opposed to the state, and knew that the things he got from the state were essentially criminal because the authority that was granted him did not originate in the permission of those who claimed to govern him. Similarly, the white race, and those of the Arya who continue to struggle and strive against the destruction of the world that has been wrought by the culture-destroyers, must know that our ability to act is neither dictated nor constrained by the desires of the governments that exert their tyranny over us. We do not need the permission of the culture destroyers to act or to publish as long as we can exert by force or ruse the ability to do so. The laws that the Jews and the Masons and the poisoners seek to impose upon us are as nothing to us except insofar as they are backed by force—and, when they are backed by force, we must recognize that their only legitimacy comes through force.

I was once a person who believed in peaceful political change and the promise of democracy. I believed in that until I was arrested by the Marxists and brutalized because I refused to lie publicly and admit to involvement in a non-existent white supremacist-terrorist underground. During my imprisonment—and long before that, from the first day I began to speak out against the exploitation of the white American workers by the Jews and the bosses—the press libeled me viciously, parroting the lies of the communist ruling caste, and did everything they could to obscure both the true reasons for my arrest and the true circumstances of my confinement, though all of this was known to them. What I learned during the two and half years that I was tortured by the black Marxist government was that almost all of the prosecutions initiated by that government, and almost all that is said about supposed criminals by the Jews in their press, is a lie. That even the most common drug crimes, for which Negroes are imprisoned by the hundreds of thousands, are often fabrications, and that all political crimes and crimes of so-called "terrorism" involve make-believe plots, mostly ones created by the government, and the arrest and forced confessions of stooges. Nothing that the government and its press tells us about the state of affairs in this country, or in the world, is real—all of it is an elaborate and orchestrated fiction—and there is nothing that can be done to change the minds of the culture destroyers or to bring them and their instruments of power into accordance with the truth. They can be fought and murdered, or one can surrender to them.

In the 1960s, those among the white movement who embraced the violent murder of the enemies of the white race were along the right path, but they mostly acted as they did for the wrong motives—the men they recruited were often deviants or sociopaths. Yet our enemies maintain a military comprised primarily of deviants and sociopaths, and do not hesitate to wield the most violent tortures against those foolish enough to act against it peacefully. Thus I conclude that one is permitted, in the struggle against the Dark Age forces, to wield Dark Age weapons—to use criminal activities, particularly acts of criminal violence, against those whose system of governance is itself a crime. "Crime," after all, is nothing but a term used to denounce violence that is not sanctioned by the state, and thus it is a moral nullity—it is a term used by one group to de-legitimize the violence of a group with which it is in competition, while reserving to itself the right to use unlimited violence.

The use of Dark Age weapons against the forces of the Dark Age is a contradiction, and one that cannot be resolved. There is no other meaningful way to struggle, yet the means chosen for the struggle furthers the decomposition of the rotten corpse of international democracy. Acts of violence are used to feed the propaganda of the enemy—yet the enemy will eventually achieve the same goals even if it is denied such propaganda material. Because no one can stop the forward march of time, and no one can stop the destruction it inevitably brings, nothing that can be done can stop the demonic forces from consuming the earth, and thus every action in this world contains within it the seeds for the furtherance of the evil agenda.

Because one cannot avoid furthering the agenda of the enemy, one should not try to do so. Death is the only weapon that can be meaningfully wielded against the enemies of humanity, because the enemies of humanity are only physical beings—their souls having been sacrificed and consumed by their evil gods—and thus death is the weapon that must be wielded. As each of us seeks to embody Vishnu, the Creator, we must also participate in the dance of Shiva, the Destroyer. Our enemies are able to destroy all of that we create—I had only to look what had become of the neighborhood into which I had invested millions of my money for redevelopment after I had been imprisoned to see that nothing that one does has any permanence or meaning. I believed in creating good things for other people, and I bought and rebuilt houses to provide decent, livable housing for the poor and working class; when I was released, the houses into which I had invested years of my life and millions of my dollars had been destroyed by the very people they had been designed to serve, all instigated by the hatred of the Jews and their government—and, no matter what scale I had acted upon, the result would have been the same. No act of creation goes unpunished by the forces of destruction, and thus, while we can strive to create and to do good for others, all that we create is temporal—in time—and destined to be overturned. The only act that the Jews and the serpents cannot undo is the final act of destruction—the murder of one of their demonic cohorts—and it is in such acts that real resistance to the rule of Seth-Typhon is found.

In the Bhagavad-Gita, Krishna stands with the warrior Arjuna before a horde of enemy soldiers and tells him that "Even if you do not fight, all of the warriors before you will die. Therefore, go into battle in their midst and slay them without remorse." Similarly, all of humanity from the moment of birth is doomed to death. Aryan prophecy tells us that there will come a time when all of humanity will meet that death together, and, after that point the earth will be cleansed and a way will be made for good men to live once again in peace. Until that time comes, there is no path of peaceful coexistence with the enemies of humanity. There is only constant war—a one-sided war waged by them if we refuse to join it—and the recognition of that constant war, and our constant obligation to destroy the persons, the property and the institutions of our enemies. By fulfilling this obligation we find eternal life; when we submit to them or find legitimacy in their violence and their state, we deny ourselves the immortality of our souls.

The essence of the Aryan warrior spirit is sacrifice, and, by recognizing that part of each of our own nature exists within time, and thus is subject to the same destruction that we are called to visit upon others, it is easier to reconcile ourselves to our own pending dissolution. Lesser living beings seek to perpetuate their existence eternally within time, but one of the initiatic truths taught to the ancient Arya was that the surrender of the part of one's self that is temporal is the only true path to immortality. Those who seek comfort above truth and seek to preserve their existence without creating a space in which that existence can be meaningful are base cowards—and typical of the mainstream of the modern white movement.

Unfortunately, there is no future in the white "movement" of modern times, insofar as it is a movement that is designed to perpetuate itself within the framework of democracy, or that it exists to meet secondary ends, such as providing a social network for its participants. It is nice to socialize and listen to music—and, for some, to drink beer—but that is not revolutionary or transcendent action. And it is nice to make money and to write and to talk, but that is also not revolutionary or transcendent action. Such things may complement a revolutionary movement, but they are not a revolutionary movement.

The transcendence of the individual being in a world in which the higher individual is given no place begins with at least a period of purification of one's inner being through the adoption of taboos on one's behavior. The abandonment of eating meat, for instance, is often chosen to show the respect that one has for healthy life and the disrespect one has for unhealthy life—by refusing to eat lesser specimens of animals or animals that one does not know were properly dedicated to the gods before their sacrifice. The abandonment of kosher food and food that has been cursed by the Jews is another frequent taboo. Abandonment of alcohol or mind-altering drugs, or the limitation of their use to the furtherance of extreme states in service to the greater ideal, as some have suggested that LSD be used to make one more effective in the murder of the enemies of humanity, is another limitation one might place on one's behavior. These taboos are used primarily to contain control over one's self and to give one's self victory in the greater holy war—the war to bring one's body and lesser impulses into the control of one's spirit—in order to further victory in the lesser holy war—the war to bring the enemies of the Arya into submission to god's law.

After the purification of one's inner being and the preparation for action comes action itself. This action is in two forms— one, the slaying of one's enemies, and the merciful destruction of those souls who have been corrupted irretrievably by the poison of modernity; and, two, the creation, insofar as is possible, of goodness, of proper relations and of right institutions, and the assistance and healing of those men and women who are suffering from the poison of Jewish modernism. The act of slaying the enemies of humanity is the greater of the two acts for the development of the individual soul, because it is the process of bringing into submission the fear of destruction and of pursuit by other men that accompanies the destruction of the life of the evil that is the true inner victory of such acts. With the act comes, too, the death of one's enemies and the invocation of the Victory, whose cult must be restored to pave the way for the restoration of the Aryan father. Each act of victory in battle, whether that battle is called "war'" or called "murder," is an act in furtherance of the Aryan spirit.

With purification in victory comes also the purification that must come in the inevitable defeat. Time is the great destroyer and it is destined to destroy the life in this world of every man.

Death is unavoidable; only what comes before death is subject
to our will. Every quest for virtue, no matter how pure the life
of the man, ends with death, sometimes preceded by injury,
torture, or imprisonment. In each circumstance, the individual
has the opportunity to bring the body into submission to the
soul, and to refuse to allow one's self to be destroyed mentally
by that which destroys one physically.

In practice, this is virtually impossible during the act of destruction itself. Only repeated experience of torture and brutality can inure one to torture and brutality, and such repeated
experience tends to scar and degrade the soul. The individual
who can maintain the purity and the benevolence of the Arya
toward the innocent after having experienced the torture that
the forces of evil and the men who submit to them inflict and
permit is rare indeed.

During my own imprisonment, right until the end, when I
had truly lost everything, I was a fool, and often believed that the
acts taken against me, which seemed to be so insensible, were a
mistake. I could not believe that people whose job, I foolishly
believed, was to uphold the law, could be abusing me knowing
that I was innocent of any violation of the law. I also could not
believe that such individuals could not hold the law as something more sacred than their own interests and the evil principles to which they had devoted their souls.

I also could not believe that the men and women I had depended upon to support me in a time of need—people I
thought valued me or valued our common struggle—would
abandon me or exploit me and my memory in the manner they
did. What I learned is that the human race, even those inclined
toward the best principles, are a race of cowards who care only
for prolonging their misery in this world, as long as it could be
prolonged. Though many knew I was innocent, in the face of a
government that they believed was "unbeatable," they were

willing not only to abandon me, but to abandon the principles upon which their relationship with me was based, rather than accept the revelation about themselves that their cowardly behavior compelled, or to accept that revelation about society and the demands upon their behavior that such revelations brought. The best of my friends literally fled the country rather than give truthful evidence in my defense, citing their fear of physical injury, arrest, or imprisonment; my own wife chose to destroy everything I had owned, then our marriage and our family, rather than accept the reality that she lived in a world where almost unlimited power was wielded by evil men.

I also saw how the system protected true criminals—low men, mentally ill and violent men, who were willing to engage in any sort of predation—as long as those true criminals acted in the system's interest. Increasingly, I came to realize that the system, from the president to the lowest of bureaucrats, was comprised of evil men.

Eventually there came a time when the government acknowledged, in its conversations with my attorneys, my innocence, even citing it in a "generous" offer to release me if I would agree to lie about "white supremacist terrorism" to further its political ends. When the offer was refused, the government communicated clearly that if I was innocent, that was all the more reason to torture and abuse me, because to release me without my repentance and submission to the Jews' will would be to admit that the government was wrong and that the Jews behind it were not all powerful.

By the time I came to realize the nature of the system that I had once believed in, it was too late for me. Had I not had the fortune of finding an honest judge who ordered me released, the government would have had its way—and I would have been sustained for decades for the purpose of abuse and torture until my inevitable "natural" death. The fact that the demonic government of Jewish America does not hesitate to sustain and torture men for decades should be enough in and of itself to justify and incite armed rebellion against it and the murder of all of its officials, particularly those involved directly in law enforcement, prosecution, the judiciary and corrections—the direct instruments of such abuse. Yet the people of the United States prefer to turn their heads away from the darkness of the communist regime that controls them and gaze only upon the petty nothingness of their disintegrated and individuated lives. And those who do look gladly latch on to one of the ideologies of justification provided for them by the Jews—even when they know form their own experience that such ideologies are a lie—because they have to lie to and pervert—poison—themselves in order to suppress their better instincts and not act.

Because essentially all of humanity participates in this unending destruction of the "best of the goyim" that is practiced by America, by the international system in which America participates, and the Jews controlling that system, essentially all of humanity can be held accountable for it, and the moral basis for the destruction of the entirety of the human race is there set. Prophecy tells us that the earth is going to burn when the last Arya is destroyed and the heavens open with the armies of Valhalla, and to anticipate that destruction by the annihilation of any number of men and women who participate in the maintenance of the existing system of demonic and Jewish rule is permissible and legitimate.

Few reading this will ever heed these words, because the nature of living beings is to sustain themselves in any condition of slavery, but the few reading it who do are the only ones whose lives and souls matter, because they are the last of the Arya that our brethren are awaiting, eagerly, in Valhalla, pending the day of vengeance and the final destruction of the Satanic race. It is imperative that the last seats at Odin's hall be filled, because the end of the world must be brought about so that those few good men, women and children who have died in innocence can be resurrected and the Golden Age reborn.

I write these truths without any fear, though I know I am the target of the death forces—their greatest target, at least in my small region of the country—and that I will, in time, be again imprisoned and eventually murdered for the truths I have shared. The things I am expressing are not a personal opinion or an expression of my will—I did not wake up one morning and decide I wanted to see mankind destroyed for my benefit. They are an expression of an eternal truth that cannot be stopped by any means. No matter what is done to me, no matter how these words are suppressed, the fate of mankind has been sealed since the first war entered the world and the vales of the eddying mead were abandoned by the gods. I am doomed to destruction as are all men, and there are, ultimately, no "consequences" for any act I take that does not blemish my soul. Really, in many ways I have transcended the notions of good and evil—the pure materiality—that allows for blemish upon the soul. Having been at the bottom, and been at a peak of creative joy, I realize that there is nothing in this world but the unending now and the march toward destruction and rebirth that that now experiences.

I write this afterword, which may never see print, in the knowledge that no book, written and printed, ever truly dies. Words that are written live forever—sometimes in their original form, and sometimes in the impressions that they leave upon others. As I have learned more of what occurred in ancient times, and seen the power that the most inane writings of 5,000 years ago have upon today, I sometimes reflect what the scribe who impressed his reed pen in the clay tablets of Uruk, recording cattle transactions in the days just before the burning of his city, would have thought if he had known the impact those writings would have upon the men of a society he could only imagine in the remnants of the prophecy left to him by the ancient Aryan gods. Similarly, I look at the words of those who came before me, and the impact they have had upon me and upon so many others, and I realize that, no matter what abuse the individual suffers, or what acts the individual takes, the well-written word lives on until it finds fertile soul and throws out new roots from which to grow to its fruition.

I can only hope this record of the destruction of mankind, in the name of evil gods and demonic rituals, can live on past my own destruction, and that the memory of what these evil men did in my time can be cause for future generations to reflect on the evil that may encroach upon their times. The men that live upon the Earth in my lifetime are all doomed, as is the society in which I have been raised and in which I write. But there will come a time when there is a society that is not doomed that can look upon history and understand what the Jews and their evil allies were able to create—and to guard against these sleeping monsters so that they may never again awaken and threaten the Arya and the human race.

WILLIAM WHITE

William A. "Bill" White is the former Commander of the American National Socialist Workers Party, one of the best organized groups that advocated for the rights of white working people in the era before the ascension of the black communist government to power in the United States. A disciple of Julius Evola and Savitri Devi, he has been cited by Jewish and anti-racist groups as the loudest and most effective advocate for National Socialism and an end to Jewish power in the United States.

Selected as a patsy by the American intelligence community, he was arrested in October 2008 and brutalized for two and a half years in an effort to make him confess to a government-contrived plot to assassinate then-candidate Barack Obama with a truck bomb. When White refused to confess, despite offers of early release and an end to torture, he was indicted five times on charges ranging from murder, kidnap and extortion to witness intimidation and transmitting threats. He was acquitted in April 2011 after a Court ruled government officials had lied, presented perjured evidence to a Grand Jury, arrested White without probable cause and wrongfully imprisoned him for 30 months. Despite this finding, the federal government continues to pursue White, accusing him—despite having repeatedly admitted in court to having "no evidence" to support these allegations—of orchestrating the 2007 kidnapping of Elie Wiesel and the 2005 murder of the family of U.S. District Judge Joan Lefkow, as well as "15 to 20" other politically motivated killings of U.S. law enforcement and intelligence personnel and government officials.

Currently living in rural Southwest Virginia, White is retired from politics, but writes weekly for AMERICAN FREE PRESS newspaper and is a regular contributor to THE BARNES REVIEW history magazine. His case continues in appellate courts as he seeks justice and reparations for the losses his business and family suffered due to the federal government's false arrest and malicious prosecution of him. He is pursuing a degree focused on ancient history—particularly Classical and Near Eastern Studies—as he investigates the ancient Tradition and Aryan history and spirituality. He is now preparing to publish two books, one a commentary on Saxo Grammaticus' *Gesta Danorum*, and the other a brief history of the Jewish and Aryan influence on ancient Egypt.

BIBLIOGRAPHY

Devi, Savitri. *The Lightning and the Sun*. Originally published 1958. Available from THE BARNES REVIEW. I recommend reading an unabridged edition.

Evola, Julius. *Revolt Against The Modern World*. 1995, Inner Traditions Publishing. Originally published 1934.

Hitler, Adolf. *My New Order*. Reynal and Hitchcock, 1943.

Men Among The Ruins. Goodwin, Jocelyn, trans. 2002, Inner Traditions Publishing. Originally published 1953.

Rydberg, Viktor. *Teutonic Mythology*. Vol I, published in three volumes. Anderson, Rasmus, trans. Norreona Publishing, 1907. Originally published 1886.

Sturlason, Snorri. *Prose Edda*. Byock, Jesse, trans. Penguin Classics 2006. Originally published 12th century.

Teutonic Mythology. Vol II, published in two volumes. Reaves, William, trans. iUniverse Inc. 2004. Originally published 1889.

Uncredited. *The Protocols of The Learned Elders of Zion*. Marsden, Victor, trans. 2011, Rivercrest Publishing. Originally published 1903. Available from THE BARNES REVIEW.

Unknown. *Mahabharata*. Smith, John, trans. Penguin Classics 2009. Original publication in antiquity. Note that the Bhagavadgita is a portion of the Mahabharata.

Unknown. *Poetic Edda*. Larrington, Caroyle, trans. Oxford World Classics 2009. Originally published 12th century. Note that this translation has serious issues, though it is the most widely distributed in English.

FURTHER READING:

From the Temple To the Talmud: Exploring Judaic Origins, History, Folklore and Tribal Traditions. By Dr. Harrell Rhome. Softcover, 261 pages, #606, *$25*. Published by TBR.

The Work of All Ages: The Ongoing Plot to Rule the World from Biblical Times to the Present. This book is a brief history of the Jewish people, from the days of Abraham to the present. Softcover, 230 pages, #585, *$25*. Published by THE BARNES REVIEW.

An Illustrated Guide to Adolf Hitler and the Third Reich. By Stephen Goodson. This pictorial guide with accompanying text gives readers insight into the real Adolf Hitler. Softcover, oversized 8.5-by-11-inch format, 40 pages, #528. 1-9 copies are *$15* each. 6-20 are *$12* each. 20 or more are just *$10* each. Published by THE BARNES REVIEW.

The Controversy of Zion. By Douglas Reed with preface by Ivor Benson. Discusses the long tentacles of Zionism. Softcover, 587 pages, #375, *$22.50*. Published by TBR.

Dissecting the Holocaust: The Growing Critique of 'Truth' and 'Memory'. Edited by Germar Rudolf. Second revised edition, softcover, 8.5" by 11", 616 pages, B&W illustrations, bibliography, index, #219, *$30*. Published by THE BARNES REVIEW.

A Straight Look at WWII. This special theme issue of THE BARNES REVIEW for January/February 2012 is a great primer for anyone interested in WWII. Prices are as follows: One to five copies are *$8* each; six or more are just *$5* each.

Revenge of the Neanderthal. Special theme issue of THE BARNES REVIEW for May/June 2010. "Revenge of the Neanderthal" is a provocative study of what may well be the most explosive anthropological secret of all time. Prices are as follows: One to five copies are *$8* each; six or more are just *$5* each.

In the maverick tradition of one of the great historians of the modern era . . .

TBR ORDERING COUPON TBR subscribers take 10% off book prices

Item #	Description/Title	Qty	Cost Ea.	Total
			SUBTOTAL	
		Add S&H on books*		
Send me a 1-year subscription to TBR for $46**				
Send me a 2-year subscription to TBR for $78**				
			TOTAL	

*S&H ON BOOKS: Add $5 S&H on orders up to $50. Add $10 S&H on orders from $50.01 to $100. Add $15 S&H on orders over $100. Outside the U.S. double these S&H charges.

TBR SUBSCRIPTION PRICES: U.S.A: $46 one year; $78 two years. **Canada/Mexico: $65 per year. **ALL OTHER NATIONS:** $80 per year delivered via air mail.

PAYMENT OPTIONS: ❏ CHECK/MO ❏ VISA ❏ MC ❏ AMEX ❏ DISCOVER

Card # _____

Expiration Date _____   Signature _____

CUSTOMER INFORMATION:

Name _____

Address _____

City/State/Zip _____

RETURN WITH PAYMENT TO: THE BARNES REVIEW, P.O. Box 15877, Washington, D.C. 20003. Call 1-877-773-9077 toll free to charge to major credit cards.

COR12

The Work of All Ages

The Ongoing Plot to Rule the World from Biblical Times to the Present

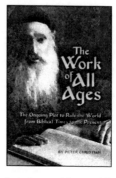

This book is a brief history of the Jewish people, from the days of Abraham to the present. The Jews are a very intelligent group, hard working and well organized, but are often resented, despised and persecuted.

From ancient times, they have had a vision of Jewish world supremacy, based on the belief that they are God's "chosen people." Today they look forward to the coming of the Jewish messiah, who will lead them to rule the world from Jerusalem. The state of Israel—in Jewish eyes the reincarnation of the legendary kingdoms of Solomon and David—however, has no problem with targeting the great Christian and Muslim centers of the world with nuclear weapons if it is threatened with destruction before this comes about, i.e., "the Samson Option."

In 33 chapters, this book reviews some of the things the Jews have done over the centuries—often in great secrecy—to advance this agenda. Included are the following: the conquest of Canaan; unity in dispersion; development of the Talmud and Kabbalah; conversion of the Khazars to Judaism; support of the Protestant reformation; development of Freemasonry; institution of central banking systems; the Rothschild Protocols; the creation of Order of the Illuminati; the creation of the Sabbatean sect—worship of Lucifer; the development of Communism and Zionism; the Protocols of the Learned Elders of Zion; the Bolshevik overthrow of the Christian czar in Russia; the creation of the Frankfurt School in Germany and the foisting of Cultural Marxism on the peoples of the Western world; control of the media; formation of the state of Israel; the infiltration and undermining of the Vatican; the globalization movement; and the institution of the so-called "New World Order."

CPSIA information can be obtained at www.ICGtesting.com
Printed in the USA
LVOW120939040512

280335LV00002B/3/P

9 781937 787059